"Just like Mary in the Bible, Mary J. Nelson has learned to sit at the feet of Jesus. As a breast cancer survivor she has walked through the valley and knows the feelings and fears. For those on a similar journey, her words will bring humor and hope, peace and power. Her counsel will seem so personal and will provide a measure of *grace for each hour.*"

—Bill Bohline
  Lead pastor, Hosanna! Lutheran Church

"*Grace for Each Hour* reminds you that you are not alone. Mary's inspirational devotions come from someone who has been there—and you feel as though she is speaking directly to you— helping you with each step. It is a book that can be revisited time and time again—both during treatment and continuing on as a survivor. Mary helps you release the fear into God's hands— reminding you to live a life with purpose, love, hope, and faith. Her encouragement through faith and a positive attitude will help sustain you through your journey."

—Vicki Steindel
  Breast cancer survivor

"Any woman who has or has had breast cancer will relate to Mary's open and honest accounts of her personal experience. Reading this book reminds me that God is always with me. The words lessen my fears and strengthen my faith."

—Elaine Buechner
  Breast cancer survivor

"Mary J. Nelson, a truly remarkable individual, takes you on a journey of growing faith in the face of crisis. This is an exquisitely written book about the strength of faith in helping pass through a time of fear, confusion, and physical weakness. Well done and a good read for anyone."

—John H. Brown, M.D.
  Medical oncologist

GRACE *for* EACH HOUR

MARY J. NELSON

BETHANY HOUSE
Minneapolis, Minnesota

Published by Bethany House Publishers
11400 Hampshire Avenue South
Bloomington, Minnesota 55438

Bethany House Publishers is a division of
Baker Publishing Group, Grand Rapids, Michigan.

Printed in the United States of America

Library of Congress Cataloging-in-Publication Data

Nelson, Mary J. (Mary Jeanne).
    Grace for each hour : through the breast cancer journey / by Mary J. Nelson.
    p. cm.
    Summary: "A devotional written to be a part of a woman's journey from diagnosis, through treatment, and survival of breast cancer"—Provided by publisher.
    ISBN 0-7642-0024-0 (pbk.)
    1. Breast—Cancer—Patients—Prayer-books and devotions—English. 2. Christian women—Prayer-books and devotions—English. I. Title.
    BV4910.33.N45   2005
    242'.4—dc22
                                               2004024238

To my husband, Howie,
who has loved me in sickness and in health,
with hair and without; to my God who binds us
together; and to His Son who set me free.

MARY J. NELSON is the president and founder of Soterion, a healthcare communications consulting firm, and she serves on the vision board at Hosanna! Lutheran Church in Lakeville, Minnesota. She is currently vice-president of the 5,000-member congregation, where she also leads the Pray for the Cure cancer care ministry. As a breast cancer survivor and a woman with a heart for prayer, Mary also serves as an intercessor and one-on-one mentor for women with breast cancer. Mary and her husband have two adult children and make their home in Minnesota.

ACKNOWLEDGMENTS

For helping me make this book a reality, I thank God for:

My parents, Ray and Jeanne Hangge, who planted the seeds of faith in my heart.

Pastors Bill Bohline and Pat Moe, the prayer team, and other leaders of Hosanna! in Lakeville, Minnesota, who nurtured the seeds, tended to the harvest, and equipped me for this ministry.

My small groups: Bob and Carolyn Sjoquist, Steve and Linda Hurst, and Mike and Julie Swecker of Kalifornia Kids, Hosanna! Bikers, 5Bs, and especially my fellow WPs Mary Carroll, Julie Swecker, and Barb Wilson who hold me to my calling, teach me how to love, cover me with prayer, and always make me laugh.

Ann Parrish of Bethany House Publishers, who recognized the need, encouraged me through countless e-mails, and never gave up on this project.

Kyle Duncan, Julie Smith, Tim Peterson, Teresa Fogarty, Brett Benson, and the entire Bethany House family, for using their amazing creative talents and wisdom to glorify our heavenly Father, for believing in me, and for helping me bring hope to the suffering.

My parents-in-law, Phil and Charlotte Nelson, who welcomed me into their home and into their hearts.

My brother, Mark Hangge, and my sister, Marilyn Kiser, who loved and supported me throughout my cancer journey.

My husband, Howie, our son, Bryan, daughter, Kelly, and daughter-in-law, Sharmi, who fill me with joy and show me grace every day.

CONTENTS

THEN I HEARD THE LORD ASKING, "WHOM
SHOULD I SEND AS A MESSENGER TO MY
PEOPLE? WHO WILL GO FOR US?" AND I
SAID, "LORD, I'LL GO! SEND ME."
Isaiah 6:8

PREFACE

ord, I'll go! Send me. I cried their tears. I felt their pain. I know every fear. I understand their broken hearts.

On August 18, 1999, my life changed forever. On that day, the Lord reached out His hand and gave me two choices. I could face breast cancer on my own, or I could trust Him. I took His hand and held on for dear life. For the next several months, He gently led me on a remarkable journey of spiritual awakening. For the first time in my life, my relationship with Jesus Christ became real and personal. He brought me into the throne room of God. He brought me face-to-face with His holiness and my own brokenness. He used the refining fire of breast cancer to purify my heart and soul. And then He sent me to tell you . . .

🌿 You are not alone (Psalm 139:1–18).

🌿 The God who made you will never fail you (1 Peter 4:19).

🌿 He has not forgotten you (Isaiah 44:21).

🌿 He delights in you (Psalm 37:23–24).

🌿 He was, and is, and always will be the God who restores your health and heals your wounds (Jeremiah 30:17).

Right now, the darkness of cancer may be closing in. Hope may seem beyond your reach. But with God in the center, this devastating diagnosis can become a precious blessing that will transform your life forever. The book you hold in your hands is a personal testimony of God's amazing grace, how it carried me through breast cancer, and how it can carry you. I pray each devotion will speak the promises of God into your heart and meet you exactly at your point of need. I pray you will see with your eyes, hear with your ears, understand with your heart, and turn to Him for healing. May the love of Christ fill your heart. May His perfect peace bring comfort to your soul. And may your Father in heaven give you grace for each hour of the journey.

BEFORE YOU BEGIN

*T*he book you hold in your hands is not about breast cancer. You won't learn about breast anatomy, causes of cancer, how breast cancer is diagnosed, or the multitude of treatment options. This is a book about our heavenly Father, His unfailing love, and His amazing grace. Breast cancer is simply a tool He will use to draw us closer to Him and bring us into a deeper relationship with His Son. Perhaps, through the pain of breast cancer, God has your undivided attention. He certainly had mine. Perhaps it has deepened your hunger for Him. If so, the words in this book will provide nourishment for your soul.

Breast cancer will take you on a roller coaster ride of emotion from the time cancer is suspected, to the end of the long treatment cycle, and in the weeks and months that follow. *Grace for Each Hour* contains 120 devotions that tenderly speak God's Word into some of the thoughts, fears, and feelings you might experience. The devotions are not organized in any particular order. You may pick up the book at any point in your journey. You might read it cover to cover, or you might let God lead you to a particular message He has planned for that day. Perhaps you'll want to read one devotion each weekday to comfort and sustain you throughout a typical six-month breast cancer experience. Regardless of how or when you choose to open this book, always pray that God will open your heart to what He wants to show you.

Be sure to keep your Bible at your side as you read and meditate on the words you read. You will find a key verse at the beginning of each reading and several Bible references woven throughout the text. You'll be surprised how God blesses you as you dig deeper into His Word for further study. I recommend a good study Bible in either the New Living Translation (NLT) or New International Version (NIV). Most of the Scripture references in this book are from the New Living Translation. This version is particularly easy to read and understand, especially if you are unfamiliar with the Bible or new to Bible study.

As God reveals himself to you through these devotions, you may feel a stirring deep within your spirit. I certainly did as I wrote each one. You may find yourself laughing one minute and crying the next. At times joy, peace, and hope will overflow from the depths of your soul. Other times you might feel troubled, impatient, angry, or perplexed. It's okay. God is with you in this journey. He's been with you all along. He never left your side. Your feelings and struggles don't surprise Him. If you keep a journal, write down any thoughts or prayers stirring in your heart. What a blessing to look back and praise God for the battles He has won, the wisdom He has given you, the prayers He has answered, and the grace He has poured on you!

Yes, His grace *is* amazing. How sweet the sound! His grace is the source of all good things . . . peace, strength, love, faith, and all His glorious blessings from heaven. His grace is powerful. It was grace that caused the whole building to shake when the apostles prayed for the power to do miracles in the name of Jesus. God answered their prayer and poured His great grace upon them (Acts 4:29–31, 33). Grace so powerful, it enabled them to perform many miraculous signs and wonders among the people. Grace so powerful that all the sick people brought before them were healed (Acts 5:12, 16). And now it's time to let His grace wash over you like a gentle rain. Make yourself comfortable and give the Lord your full attention. Let the healing begin. 🌿

THROUGH THE VALLEY

> TRUST IN THE LORD WITH ALL YOUR
> HEART; DO NOT DEPEND ON YOUR OWN
> UNDERSTANDING. SEEK HIS WILL IN ALL YOU
> DO, AND HE WILL DIRECT YOUR PATHS.
> DON'T BE IMPRESSED WITH YOUR OWN
> WISDOM. INSTEAD, FEAR THE LORD AND
> TURN YOUR BACK ON EVIL. THEN YOU WILL
> GAIN RENEWED HEALTH AND VITALITY.
> *Proverbs 3:5–8*

*T*he words of the surgeon are forever etched in my mind. "Your biopsy results are back and you have an invasive breast cancer. . . ." I was too stunned to scream or cry or ask *why me.* Besides, my journey had already begun several weeks earlier. A scheduling miscue had made it possible for me to make a first-time appointment with a reputable area doctor even though she was booked a year out and not accepting new patients. During her routine exam, she found a mildly suspicious area on my left breast. My mammogram showed nothing, but just to be sure, she ordered more tests.

During the agonizing time between tests, I read every scientific article and book on breast cancer I could get my hands on, as if my knowledge and understanding would somehow allow me to control the situation. But as my knowledge increased, so did my fear. Fear soon turned to panic until finally on the day before that fateful phone call, I fell to my knees and cried out to God in total desperation. I felt a supernatural peace come over me I had never felt before. I knew at that moment God was in the middle of this cancer. He was in control, whatever the outcome.

As I think back to that day, I remember how the words I had memorized as a child in Sunday school played over and over in my mind. *Yea, though I walk through the valley of the shadow of death, I will fear no evil: for thou art with me; thy rod and thy staff they comfort me* (Psalm 23:4 KJV). I clung to those words. *I'm not alone. He has not abandoned me. I have nothing to fear. He will comfort me through this valley.*

I never believed the Lord gave me breast cancer. But I knew He planned to use it somehow for His purposes. He causes *all* things to work together for the good of those who love Him (Romans 8:28). So I made a decision that day to walk through the valley with God and trust the words I had memorized as a child. He had already led me to right doctors, cleared their schedules, and guided them into making a diagnosis that easily could have been missed. I would continue to trust Him to direct my path.

What path will you take through the valley of cancer? You can push God away. You can try to research your way out and put all your hope in scientific knowledge. Or you can choose the path of trust and follow Him. There's more power in God than in all the world's wisdom. So don't depend on your own understanding and stumble through the valley on your own. Let Him direct your path. He'll lead the way to renewed health and vitality! That's a promise. ❦

HE GOES FIRST

> O LORD, YOU HAVE EXAMINED MY HEART
> AND KNOW EVERYTHING ABOUT ME. YOU
> KNOW WHEN I SIT DOWN OR STAND UP.
> YOU KNOW MY EVERY THOUGHT WHEN FAR
> AWAY. YOU CHART THE PATH AHEAD OF ME
> AND TELL ME WHERE TO STOP AND REST.
> EVERY MOMENT YOU KNOW WHERE I AM.
> YOU KNOW WHAT I AM GOING TO SAY EVEN
> BEFORE I SAY IT, LORD. YOU BOTH PRECEDE
> AND FOLLOW ME. YOU PLACE YOUR HAND
> OF BLESSING ON MY HEAD. . . . YOU SAW ME
> BEFORE I WAS BORN. EVERY DAY OF MY LIFE
> WAS RECORDED IN YOUR BOOK. EVERY
> MOMENT WAS LAID OUT BEFORE
> A SINGLE DAY HAD PASSED.
> *Psalm 139:1–5, 16*

It took at least a week before it all sank in. Cancer. The word itself was surreal. Surely there was some huge mistake. Cancer happened to *other* people. Besides, I had healthy relatives with long life-spans and no breast cancer history. During the whirlwind week that followed my initial diagnosis, I walked around in a daze from doctor appointment to doctor appointment and one test to another. As I sifted through a mountain of information trying to make sense of my treatment options, I felt completely detached from the circumstances around me—as if someone else was going through the motions, not me. I've heard what being in shock is like, and I'm fairly sure I was in shock.

While cancer may have stunned me, it did not catch God by

surprise. He promised to always precede me in every situation. He laid out every moment of my life and charted every path ahead of me before a single day had passed. He knows every thought before I think it and every word before I say it. He not only went before me into my battle against cancer, He went beside me and behind me. When the fog lifted around me, I could see His perfect plan unfold in every situation I encountered. He provided resources to guide every decision from doctors and drugs to hats and wig suppliers. He gave me shoulders to lean on, ears willing to listen, and hearts to pray for my every need. He protected me and comforted me through each phase of treatment (Psalm 91; 139:7–12).

As you prepare to fight your battle today, remember this: Jesus Christ went before you and He has a battle plan. He knows every fear, every question, and every doubt that will rise up within you before *you* do. He went ahead of you to scout the territory. He has already cleared a pathway through the rough and rocky terrain that lies ahead. He will give you everything you need to get through it at precisely the time you need it most. You can march on with bold confidence. He has you covered from all directions. 🌾

ENJOY THE RIDE

CONFESS YOUR SINS TO EACH OTHER AND
PRAY FOR EACH OTHER SO THAT YOU MAY
BE HEALED. THE EARNEST PRAYER OF A
RIGHTEOUS PERSON HAS GREAT POWER AND
WONDERFUL RESULTS.

James 5:16

As I opened my eyes in the recovery room, I could barely make out the face of the surgeon who had removed the cancerous lump from my breast. She tenderly reported the bad news. They found cancer in two lymph nodes under my arm. This unforeseen setback would add five months of chemotherapy to the six weeks of radiation treatments I had opted for instead of total removal of the breast.

This was *not* the news we wanted to hear, not the news we'd hoped and prayed for. But I went into surgery lifted by the prayers of an army of the faithful and righteous. Family and friends, prayer ministers from my church community, and people I'd never even met all covered me with prayer. They sent prayers in cards and letters. They e-mailed prayers. They called me and prayed with me over the phone. I was so lifted by prayer and filled with the Holy Spirit that with the bad news that day came an indescribable calmness . . . a peace far more wonderful than my human mind could understand (Philippians 4:6–7). Their prayers continued throughout my entire treatment. When my doctors, friends, and family commented on my "positive attitude," I knew it wasn't me. It was the peace and contentment of Christ showing through in answer to their prayers. It was Jesus who carried me safely through the valley in His arms and lifted me high above my physical circumstances.

The prayers of the righteous have great power and wonderful results! Don't attempt to go through this journey alone. Let the prayers of your family, friends, and a loving faith community cover and protect you. Their prayers offered in faith will heal you and the Lord will raise you up (James 5:15 NRSV). Life is taking you on a detour through the valley, so why not fall back into His arms and enjoy the ride? ❦

HOPE FOR YOUR BROKEN HEART

HE HEALS THE BROKENHEARTED,
BINDING UP THEIR WOUNDS.
Psalm 147:3

Σeptember 11 will be forever etched on our minds and hearts. I watched in horror with the rest of the nation as the events unfolded that morning on television. The feelings came flooding back, the same shock, disbelief, and anger I experienced on the day of my diagnosis. In the days and weeks that followed, we learned more about the lives that were shattered on that day. Perhaps like me, you shared a familiar pain with the victims' families—that dull ache that settles into the core of our soul as we grieve the loss of a loved one we will never see again, a way of life we fear is gone forever, or the healthy body we always took for granted—the pain of a broken heart.

But God promised to heal our broken hearts and bind our wounds. The prophet Isaiah said those who do not seek to know and understand God have hardened their hearts against Him and cannot turn to Him for healing (Isaiah 6:10). Only when our hardened hearts are broken can God shower us with righteousness (Hosea 10:12). Breast cancer broke my heart wide open. It shattered it into a million pieces. It was my brokenness that allowed the Word of God to slowly begin penetrating the depths of my heart (Proverbs 4:20–22). And it was through that brokenness that God could begin the most significant restoration project in my life.

When I think about restoration, I see the devastation at

Ground Zero and I imagine the rebuilding that takes place after any war. I'm reminded of a story I heard about a cathedral in Europe with a priceless stained-glass window that was shattered in a bombing raid. The pieces were gathered and stored until a skilled craftsman from another city learned of the damage. When he came to the village offering to restore the window, the people gave him all the pieces but held little hope he would succeed. Several months later, the craftsman returned and replaced the window in the cathedral. The people were amazed to find the restored window even more beautiful than the original. And like that shattered window, God couldn't repair my broken heart until I surrendered all the pieces.

Have you given God the pieces of your broken heart? Sometimes we hold on to our brokenness because we're not finished grieving, we're not finished being angry, or we simply don't trust Him to make us whole again. But God wants to fill the empty void you feel in the pit of your soul. He wants to send you a skilled craftsman, one who knows every piece of your shattered heart, one who knows your every pain, one who has shared in your suffering, and one who can put the pieces back together and make you well and whole and more beautiful than before (Isaiah 61:1). He wants to give you Jesus. ❦

Even Your Hairs Are Numbered

> Not even a sparrow, worth only half
> a penny, can fall to the ground
> without your Father knowing it. And
> the very hairs on your head are all
> numbered. So don't be afraid; you are
> more valuable to him than a whole
> flock of sparrows.
> *Matthew 10:29–31*

I took great comfort in knowing that God knew exactly how many hairs were on my head before chemotherapy had its way. I'm embarrassed to admit that my hair was the very first thought that came to mind when the possibility of cancer was discovered. It wasn't, "Oh, dear God, I could lose my life!" It wasn't even, "Oh, dear God, I could lose my breast!" It was, "Oh, please God, not my hair!" It was on a Monday, exactly seventeen days after my first chemo treatment, that it started falling out. At first I noticed a few strands at times on my computer keyboard and white countertops. A couple of days later it was falling out in clumps. By Thursday, I'd had enough. I called my husband at work and told him to bring home clippers. That night, my dear, sweet husband sat me down on a chair in the kitchen and, with the dog licking my feet, shaved all the remaining hair off my head. I'll never forget what he said when he was done. He told me I had a beautifully shaped head, and he meant it.

Jesus said God knows everything that happens, even to the sparrows. He knew about every strand of hair my husband shaved off my head that night. Just imagine how much more valuable we are to God than sparrows and hair! You and I are so valuable that God sent His only Son to shed His blood and redeem us from our sin. With this ultimate act of love, He gave us direct access to the very throne of God (Hebrews 4:16).

But this doesn't necessarily mean He takes away all our troubles. It means He *already* has triumphed over every trouble and every struggle we will ever face (John 16:33). It means we never need to fear threats or difficult trials again because He sent each of us a personal Savior, our own personal Counselor, and *nothing* can separate us from the Spirit of God that dwells within every believer (Romans 8:31–39). It means that the very same power that rose Christ Jesus from the dead is *within you*. It means you are far more valuable to God than a flock of sparrows or a few strands of hair. By the way, He remembered exactly how many hairs fell out of my beautifully shaped head and He restored every single one. ❦

New Beginnings

> WHAT THIS MEANS IS THAT THOSE WHO
> BECOME CHRISTIANS BECOME NEW PERSONS.
> THEY ARE NOT THE SAME ANYMORE, FOR
> THE OLD LIFE IS GONE. A NEW LIFE
> HAS BEGUN!
> *2 Corinthians 5:17*

For many of us, the start of each new year marks a new beginning. Our commitment to better health, improved finances, and more meaningful relationships shows up in the long lines for the step machines and the treadmill, enrollment in weight-loss programs, and the sale of self-improvement books. We replace the pages in our Day-Timers and make a fresh commitment to balancing our priorities.

Sometimes it takes more than a flip of the calendar page to get our attention. September 11 marked a fresh start for many Americans. The events of that day brought a nation to its knees in prayer as we were reminded of our human frailty and our total dependence on God. In the aftermath of the attacks, the compassion of people for their neighbors, the resurgence in church attendance, and a rekindled love for our country were evidence of a nation reborn.

Perhaps you didn't need a terrorist attack to turn your life in a new direction. I didn't. I needed breast cancer. In one phone call, everything I knew became uncertain. Suddenly, it mattered more to be right with God, to know Him intimately, and to be consistent in my faith. The "old me" was gone forever as I faced the future knowing that Christ was all that I needed and nothing—

not life, not death, not angels, not demons, not fears, not worries, *not cancer*—would ever separate me from His love (Romans 8:38).

What a privilege to be born into God's family, to have our slate wiped clean, and to know that whatever trial we face, we have an eternal inheritance (1 Peter 1:3–6). You don't have to wait until New Year's to begin your new life. Pray this prayer now. *Heavenly Father, forgive me, for I have made mistakes in my life, I have turned my back on you, and I have not been the person you created me to be. I accept Jesus Christ as my true Lord and Savior, and I give Him first place in my life. I receive the gift of the Holy Spirit and I surrender all of me to His will.* It's the best new beginning you'll ever have. ❦

A GREAT CALM

AS EVENING CAME, JESUS SAID TO HIS
DISCIPLES, "LET'S CROSS TO THE OTHER SIDE
OF THE LAKE." HE WAS ALREADY IN THE
BOAT, SO THEY STARTED OUT, LEAVING THE
CROWDS BEHIND (ALTHOUGH OTHER BOATS
FOLLOWED). BUT SOON A FIERCE STORM
AROSE. HIGH WAVES BEGAN TO BREAK INTO
THE BOAT UNTIL IT WAS NEARLY FULL OF
WATER. JESUS WAS SLEEPING AT THE BACK OF
THE BOAT WITH HIS HEAD ON A CUSHION.
FRANTICALLY THEY WOKE HIM UP,
SHOUTING, "TEACHER, DON'T YOU EVEN
CARE THAT WE ARE GOING TO DROWN?"
WHEN HE WOKE UP, HE REBUKED THE WIND
AND SAID TO THE WATER, "QUIET DOWN!"
SUDDENLY THE WIND STOPPED, AND THERE
WAS A GREAT CALM. AND HE ASKED THEM,
"WHY ARE YOU SO AFRAID? DO YOU STILL
NOT HAVE FAITH IN ME?"
Mark 4:35–40

When Jesus warned us we would have troubles in this
world, He wasn't kidding. In a little over a year's time,
a tree fell through my living room, my husband lost his job, and I
was diagnosed with breast cancer. As the latest storm swirled
around me, I couldn't help wondering when the Lord was finally
going to take notice. Don't you care that my nodes are positive
and the cancer could be spreading? Don't you care that they may
have to remove my breast? Don't you care that I have children and

a husband who need me? Don't you care that I have meetings to lead and parties to plan and I don't have time to be sick? Don't you care that I'm the only mom at this graduation ceremony wearing a wig? *Don't you care that I'm about to drown?*

When the disciples asked this question Jesus immediately calmed the storm and questioned their faith. We have two options when storms come and Jesus doesn't seem to hear our cries for help. Like the disciples, we can panic and assume He doesn't care. When we choose to worry, we are really saying God doesn't have the power to handle our problems and we can do it better ourselves. Before long, our boats are full of water and we're fighting for our lives.

But there's another option when panic sets in and there is nowhere else to turn. We can confess our total dependence on God. An amazing thing happens when we finally let go and trust God with our problems. We receive His peace, a gift far more wonderful than the human mind can understand (Philippians 4:7). God's peace comes from our knowing that He is in complete and total control and our future in Him is secure. His perfect peace guards our hearts against all anxiety.

Never underestimate God's power and His love for you. He's always paying attention and He knows all the violent and unexpected storms this cancer will bring. Sometimes during your journey, He will calm the fierce relentless wind swirling around you. He may send a friend with a meal or a playmate for your child on a day you simply can't get out of bed. Other times, He'll calm the silent storm raging inside your heart. Either way, there *will* be a great calm . . . regardless of the weather forecast. ❦

BEYOND YOUR WILDEST DREAMS

> I AM THE LORD, THE GOD OF ALL THE
> PEOPLES OF THE WORLD. IS ANYTHING TOO
> HARD FOR ME? . . . ASK ME AND I WILL TELL
> YOU SOME REMARKABLE SECRETS ABOUT
> WHAT IS GOING TO HAPPEN HERE.
> *Jeremiah 32:27; 33:3*

Shortly after my diagnosis I was referred to a healing coach, a healthcare professional trained in holistic approaches for treating the mind, body, and spirit of the cancer patient. Sometime during the course of our conversation about herbs, acupuncture, reflexology, and dance therapy, I started talking about prayer and my faith in God. He was conspicuously missing from the list of complementary therapies. I think I said something like, "My God has never let me down." The coach said nothing, but the expression on her face captured all the doubt and fear that filled my own heart the moment I boldly spoke those words.

Why do we doubt Him? The Israelites spent forty years wandering in the desert because they failed to trust that God would meet their current needs even though He performed incredible miracles each and every time they faced a crisis. In the same way, God promises to rescue us in times of trouble and to supply our every need (Psalm 50:15; Philippians 4:19). But we don't believe He's up to the task *this* time. Sure, Jesus healed the sick, but that was two thousand years ago. Miracles might happen today, but certainly not to anyone I know. After all, this is *cancer* we're talking about. We pray for a miracle, but then we lower our expectations of what God can do. Sometimes we're even pleasantly surprised if our prayers are answered. As a result, we wander through the desert like the Israelites, believing that God's abundant promises of care are unavailable to us . . . sort of like window shoppers who only dream about owning the expensive items behind the glass.

If you think this cancer is too much for God to handle, you're mistaken. The same God who placed the stars in the sky, parted the sea, and raised Christ from the dead can battle your cancer. You don't have to live in spiritual poverty fearing His promises are out of your reach. God's plans for you are far greater than your human mind can ever imagine. Trust the greatest Healing Coach of all time with your body, mind, and spirit, and He will use this cancer to take you places you never dreamed possible! ❧

BECAUSE I SAID SO

> "MY THOUGHTS ARE COMPLETELY
> DIFFERENT FROM YOURS," SAYS THE LORD.
> "AND MY WAYS ARE FAR BEYOND ANYTHING
> YOU COULD IMAGINE. FOR JUST AS THE
> HEAVENS ARE HIGHER THAN THE EARTH, SO
> ARE MY WAYS HIGHER THAN YOUR WAYS
> AND MY THOUGHTS HIGHER THAN
> YOUR THOUGHTS."
> *Isaiah 55:8–9*

Because I said so. I remember how much I hated to hear my parents say those four words. I vowed never to use them with my own children. I planned to give a detailed explanation every time I corrected my child, handed down a decision, or issued an order. But eventually I learned that my parents had wisdom far beyond my years, and some things just didn't need to be explained. Because I trusted them to take care of me and I knew how much they loved me, I knew their decisions were always in my best interest. It became even clearer after I had children of my own.

Isn't the same true with our heavenly Father? How many times have you heard people question Him? If there is a God, where was He on September 11? If God is so good, why do I have cancer? Why do some people die of cancer and others overcome it? How often do we reject Him because His ways don't always fit into the limits of our worldly understanding of justice and fairness?

Cancer can bring us face-to-face with God's sovereignty. With my scientific training, I like facts and figures and detailed explanations. But there are no definitive answers, medically or otherwise. I found comfort in knowing God is wise and good and His Son is a light of hope in a fallen world. I trusted His promise that something good would come out of this cancer and He would somehow use it for His purposes (Romans 8:28). But most of all, I was reminded of a lesson I learned long ago. Just as a child doesn't question his parents' wisdom, the clay doesn't question the potter's work (Romans 9:20–21). His ways are higher than mine and His thoughts are higher than mine. By surrendering myself completely to Him, I also surrendered the *need* to know why. I only need to know He said so.

The next time you wonder if God knows what He's doing, think about just how much distance is between the earth and the heavens above. A million miles? Ten million? More? That's how much more your heavenly Father sees than you see. So when you search for answers to difficult questions, and the answers don't come, trust in the Potter who made you. He's a wise and loving parent. When you ask Him, He'll tell you: *Because I said so.* ❦

A SOLID FOUNDATION

> ANYONE WHO LISTENS TO MY TEACHING
> AND OBEYS ME IS WISE, LIKE A PERSON WHO
> BUILDS A HOUSE ON SOLID ROCK. THOUGH
> THE RAIN COMES IN TORRENTS AND THE
> FLOODWATERS RISE AND THE WINDS BEAT
> AGAINST THAT HOUSE, IT WON'T COLLAPSE,
> BECAUSE IT IS BUILT ON ROCK. BUT ANYONE
> WHO HEARS MY TEACHING AND IGNORES IT
> IS FOOLISH, LIKE A PERSON WHO BUILDS A
> HOUSE ON SAND. WHEN THE RAINS AND
> FLOODS COME AND THE WINDS BEAT
> AGAINST THAT HOUSE, IT WILL FALL
> WITH A MIGHTY CRASH.
> *Matthew 7:24–27*

A few years ago a terrible storm blew through our neighborhood dropping trees, blowing off rooftops, and destroying everything in its path. A large oak tree crashed through our house, and our property was virtually covered with trees, branches, shingles, and all kinds of debris. When the cleanup was finally completed and we had time to survey the damage, we were relieved to learn we had excellent insurance to cover the extensive repairs that would be necessary in the months that followed.

Knowing and trusting Jesus and building Him into our foundation is a lot like having good homeowner's insurance. When life is calm, the foundation doesn't seem to matter much. But when crisis comes, our foundation is tested. Breast cancer stormed into my life with a vengeance and shook the very core of my soul. But

Jesus promised that anyone who listens to His teaching is like a person who builds a house on solid rock. The rains may come in torrents and the wind may beat against it, but the house won't collapse. But rocks are hard to build on, aren't they? It's hard to dig a foundation into rock. Building on sand is not nearly as tedious. Besides, there's better scenery on the beach and our friends all live there. We've heard that storms might come, but what are the chances? Sometimes we talk ourselves into cutting corners and leave ourselves vulnerable . . . sort of like a homeowner without good hazard insurance.

Did this storm catch you on rock or sand? If you're on solid rock, the wind and rain may pound against your house, but your foundation will stand up against each and every blow this cancer tries to deliver. If the ground beneath you is shaky, take heart! It's never too late to build the Word of God into your life. Start now by reading the Bible every day and seeking fellowship and prayer with other believers. Ask God to lift you out of the mud and mire and set your feet on solid ground (Psalm 40:1–2). The next time the clouds darken the sky, you'll be ready. ✴

HE LOVES YOU!

> WHAT CAN WE SAY ABOUT SUCH
> WONDERFUL THINGS AS THESE? IF GOD IS
> FOR US, WHO CAN EVER BE AGAINST US?
> SINCE GOD DID NOT SPARE EVEN HIS OWN
> SON BUT GAVE HIM UP FOR US ALL, WON'T
> GOD, WHO GAVE US CHRIST, ALSO GIVE US
> EVERYTHING ELSE? . . . AND I AM
> CONVINCED THAT NOTHING CAN EVER
> SEPARATE US FROM HIS LOVE. DEATH CAN'T,
> AND LIFE CAN'T. THE ANGELS CAN'T, AND
> THE DEMONS CAN'T. OUR FEARS FOR
> TODAY, OUR WORRIES ABOUT TOMORROW,
> AND EVEN THE POWERS OF HELL CAN'T KEEP
> GOD'S LOVE AWAY. WHETHER WE ARE HIGH
> ABOVE THE SKY OR IN THE DEEPEST OCEAN,
> NOTHING IN ALL CREATION WILL EVER BE
> ABLE TO SEPARATE US FROM THE LOVE
> OF GOD THAT IS REVEALED IN
> CHRIST JESUS OUR LORD.
> *Romans 8:31–32, 38–39*

*I*magine for a moment the leader of a rich and powerful nation so full of love and concern for helping the homeless and downtrodden that he goes to live among them in the streets of the dirtiest city. He wears rags, sifts through garbage for food, sleeps in alleys and under bridges, and listens with compassion to the details of their plight.

It sounds impossible, doesn't it? People with such incredible power and authority rarely commune with common people, let alone the outcasts of society. Yet how much *more* our heavenly Father, the King of all creation, did for us! It became so clear to me during my six months of treatment. During the Advent season, while about halfway through chemotherapy, I was awestruck at the wonder of a God who loves me so much that He would send His only Son to walk this earth and redeem me from my sin. The words "Emmanuel, God is with us" suddenly came alive with new meaning. When my treatments came to an end about the time we celebrated Easter, I was even more amazed by how much the Lord really loved me: so much that He shed his blood and died so I could be healed, so much that if I were the only person on this earth, He would have done it *just for me*.

Just think . . . the Almighty God came to live among us on earth and *nothing* in all creation, not cancer or any other trouble or calamity, will ever be able to separate you from His love. And if He is with you, who or what can ever stand against you? Perhaps you attend worship and participate in the rituals of religion, but the Son and loving Father seem far too distant. Or perhaps you've always known in your head how much God loves you. Through your cancer journey you'll come to know it in your heart. ❦

LET YOUR COMFORT OVERFLOW

PRAISE BE TO THE GOD AND FATHER OF
OUR LORD JESUS CHRIST, THE FATHER OF
COMPASSION AND THE GOD OF ALL
COMFORT, WHO COMFORTS US IN ALL OUR
TROUBLES, SO THAT WE CAN COMFORT
THOSE IN ANY TROUBLE WITH THE
COMFORT WE OURSELVES HAVE RECEIVED
FROM GOD. FOR JUST AS THE SUFFERINGS OF
CHRIST FLOW OVER INTO OUR LIVES, SO
ALSO THROUGH CHRIST OUR
COMFORT OVERFLOWS.

2 Corinthians 1:3–5 NIV

I sat in the big green chair waiting for the nurse to start my IV.
She had made several attempts to find a vein, all unsuccessful.
To take my mind off things, I looked around the sunny room.
Lining a wall of windows were people of all ages resting in green
reclining chairs like mine. Family and friends surrounded each
one, talking, reading, playing cards to pass the time, or simply
holding their hand as they received chemotherapy. Suddenly I felt
moved to pray for each person sitting in one of those big green
chairs. As my prayers made their way around the room, I stopped
at Wendy. She was young, perhaps mid-twenties, and from the
conversation she was having with her mother and sister, I knew
she had breast cancer. She was having more tests in a few days. If
the results weren't good, she had run out of options. I prayed for
Wendy that day, that night, and all week long. Sometimes I woke
up in the middle of the night and prayed for her.

The day I returned to the clinic and saw Wendy again, I was discouraged and fed up with my bald head and a treatment routine that seemed to never end. Wendy came out of the exam room with a big smile on her face as she embraced the young man who had been sitting near me in the waiting room. "It's the best news I've had in weeks," she cried. I don't know for sure what news she was celebrating, but I know that God put me in that very place at that very time to not only give me strength and encouragement but to show me that my suffering could be a blessing to others.

I was reminded that day of a close friend. Throughout her own cancer journey there was something different about her. In good times and in bad, peace and contentment always radiated from her. Just thinking about her gave me hope. I pray that the Lord will shine His light through me so I too can be a comfort to others and they will know the power and strength that comes only from God. He will do the same for you. During the weeks and months of treatment ahead, when you see no light at the end of the tunnel, let the Father of compassion and the God of all comfort sustain you. Before long His love and comfort will be overflowing to those around you! ❦

KEEP YOUR EYES ON THE PRIZE

> I HAVE FOUGHT A GOOD FIGHT, I HAVE
> FINISHED THE RACE, AND I HAVE REMAINED
> FAITHFUL. AND NOW THE PRIZE AWAITS
> ME—THE CROWN OF RIGHTEOUSNESS THAT
> THE LORD, THE RIGHTEOUS JUDGE, WILL
> GIVE ME ON THAT GREAT DAY OF HIS
> RETURN. AND THE PRIZE IS NOT JUST FOR
> ME BUT FOR ALL WHO EAGERLY LOOK
> FORWARD TO HIS GLORIOUS RETURN.
> *2 Timothy 4:7–8*

To finish a race, marathon runners understand the importance of consistent training and conditioning to build up their strength and endurance. I don't run marathons, but I do climb mountains. Every July my husband and I go mountain hiking in the heart of the Canadian Rockies. As we plan our daylong treks through the high alpine trails from our base in the secluded valley, we remember that mountain weather is extremely unpredictable. A sunny day in the low eighties can quickly turn into a blinding snowstorm at higher elevations. We go the same week every year, but we'll find the trails clean one year and covered with eight feet of snow the next. A few close calls taught us the importance of preparing physically for hours of hiking through slippery rocks and steep treacherous trails and to always carry gear in our packs to counter the variable mountain conditions. The prize when we reach our final destination—breathtaking panoramic views of glacier-clad peaks and crystal blue waters—is worth all the planning, conditioning, and hard work that goes into every hike.

Inconsistency and poor preparation are sure ways to guarantee failure for the marathon runner or mountain hiker. Yet how often do we rely on yesterday's prayer and Bible study to endure today's crisis? Before my diagnosis, I drifted back and forth in my relationship with God. But God remains constant and He wants the same consistency from us (Hebrews 13:8). He warns that we must take a firm stand and not drift away from the assurance we received when we first heard the Good News (Colossians 1:23).

Only by keeping the Word of God in our eyes, ears, and heart can we be as faithful to God as He is to us. So start training now! Don't let this cancer and the unpredictable storms it brings catch you unprepared to finish the climb. Make a commitment to daily Bible study and prayer. Ask the Holy Spirit to build up your strength and give you endurance to battle all the worldly distractions that keep your eyes from focusing on the prize. Then, behold the majesty of His glory when you reach the mountaintop!

JUST ONE DAY IN HIS COURTS

HAPPY ARE THOSE WHO ARE STRONG IN THE
LORD, WHO SET THEIR MINDS ON A
PILGRIMAGE TO JERUSALEM. WHEN THEY
WALK THROUGH THE VALLEY OF WEEPING,
IT WILL BECOME A PLACE OF REFRESHING
SPRINGS, WHERE POOLS OF BLESSING
COLLECT AFTER THE RAINS! THEY WILL
CONTINUE TO GROW STRONGER AND EACH
OF THEM WILL APPEAR BEFORE GOD IN
JERUSALEM. . . . A SINGLE DAY IN YOUR
COURTS IS BETTER THAN A THOUSAND
ANYWHERE ELSE!
Psalm 84:5–7, 10

Some experiences in this life are worth the pain. If you're a mother, you know exactly what I'm talking about. After seventeen hours of labor, you wonder, *What was I thinking?* Then they put the precious little miracle in your arms and every single contraction is erased from your memory. As the child grows up and takes you through temper tantrums, sleepless nights, and speeding tickets, you wonder how anything can give you so much heartache and so much joy at the same time.

Compared to surgery, chemo, radiation, and a bald head, a few labor pains probably seem like a cakewalk. And how could any joy possibly come out of cancer? It may seem odd to you, but I wouldn't trade my cancer experience for anything in the world. Why? Because there are certain things in this life that God can reveal to us only in the midst of adversity. There are hidden places deep in our souls He can reach only through our suffering. Here in the valley of weeping, in this secret place of refreshing springs where pools of blessings collect, we meet Almighty God face-to-face. What a privilege to stand in His courts!

As you walk through the valley of weeping today, be careful not to become bitter over your suffering. If you resent God rather than seek Him, you will miss out on all the things He wants to teach you. Only when He has your undivided attention can He reveal remarkable secrets you do not know (Jeremiah 33:3). Use this time of adversity as an opportunity to catch a little glimpse of heaven. Get to know Him intimately and He will strengthen your very soul. When it's all over, you won't miss the pain and suffering. But you *will* find joy in every single day you spent in His presence. You won't trade a single one, not for a thousand somewhere else. ❦

HURRY UP AND WAIT!

> DO NOT THROW AWAY THIS CONFIDENT
> TRUST IN THE LORD, NO MATTER WHAT
> HAPPENS. REMEMBER THE GREAT REWARD
> IT BRINGS YOU! PATIENT ENDURANCE IS
> WHAT YOU NEED NOW, SO YOU WILL
> CONTINUE TO DO GOD'S WILL. THEN YOU
> WILL RECEIVE ALL THAT HE HAS PROMISED.
> *Hebrews 10:35–36*

There was a big hurry to remove the cancer. My family wanted immediate action. After spending three solid days on the phone and a week meeting with different surgeons to explore my options, I was whisked into surgery and the lump was successfully removed. Then, time stood still. It was three weeks before chemo could begin. Add eight cycles of chemo, each three weeks apart. Top that off with six weeks of radiation. I did the math and came up with seven months plus. Add another six months for the hair to grow back, and now it's at least a year. *Okay, Lord. With your help I can do this.* I remember sitting in church one Sunday about halfway into my chemo treatments. The woman in front of me had long, dark hair about the same length and style I used to wear. I stared at the back of her head from under my short, dark wig. At that moment, twelve months may as well have been twelve years, or 120 for that matter. It felt like an eternity would pass before there was any hope of my life returning to "normal."

I learned something about patience during this journey that seemed to last forever. When trouble comes, we can turn to God in faith. We can lay all our burdens down at His feet and trust

Him to carry the entire load. But faith is only the first step. Faith paves the way for God to step in and take control of our problems. God will use the time to develop our patience and strengthen our character (James 1:2–4). It's the gift of patience that keeps the path clear until the results we are waiting for are evident. It gives our faith a chance to work.

When your patience is tested, it's easy to throw away your confident trust in the Lord. It's hard to stay on the path when the victory is so slow in coming. But if you submit to God's timing He *will* honor you. He knows the best time to change your circumstances. Don't be discouraged and abandon your faith, no matter what happens or how long it takes. Hurry up! Ask Him to bear your burdens. Then wait. Show by your patience your faith is real and receive all He has promised. ❦

No Pain, No Gain

> I WILL PRAISE YOU, LORD, FOR YOU HAVE
> RESCUED ME. YOU REFUSED TO LET MY
> ENEMIES TRIUMPH OVER ME. O LORD MY
> GOD, I CRIED OUT TO YOU FOR HELP, AND
> YOU RESTORED MY HEALTH. YOU BROUGHT
> ME UP FROM THE GRAVE, O LORD. YOU
> KEPT ME FROM FALLING INTO THE
> PIT OF DEATH.
> *Psalm 30:1–3*

Do you know any perfect people? You know who I'm talking about . . . the ones who always have everything under control. They come home every day from their perfect jobs to their perfect homes and their perfect families. You catch up on the details of their perfect problem-free lives every year in their annual Christmas letters. You may be looking at them right now in the midst of your suffering and wondering, *Why is this happening to me?*

You know what? They *do* have problems, just like you and me. Maybe they aren't battling cancer, but they're battling something. And if they really do lead perfect, problem-free lives, they may be missing out. In the Bible, perfect means completeness or maturity. Through the suffering of Jesus, God made Him a perfect leader (Hebrews 2:10). By suffering, Christ shared our human experience and became like us. Now He calls us to grow toward maturity and wholeness to become more like Him (Matthew 5:48). As we become partners with Christ in His suffering, we are being "made perfect." And because we share in His suffering, we also

47

share in His victory at Calvary (1 Peter 4:12–13; 5:10).

I know what you're thinking. It's against human nature to *want* to suffer. No one wants the pain and grief that comes with it. But consider this for a moment: without a battle, there *is* no victory. If I hadn't stood at the edge of the pit of death, if I hadn't cried out for the Lord to rescue me, if He hadn't healed me with His resurrection power, I would never have *experienced* victory in Christ. I wouldn't drop to my knees every morning in complete and total awe of His grace and His mercy. I would never have fully grasped His precious gift of life and all that He sacrificed just for me. I'm not perfect yet, and neither are you . . . but we're getting closer. 🌿

MINNESOTA SPRING

THERE IS A TIME FOR EVERYTHING, AND
A SEASON FOR EVERY ACTIVITY
UNDER HEAVEN.

Ecclesiastes 3:1

J'm a native Minnesotan. Before you conjure up visions of
blowing snow, heavy boots, and fur-trimmed hooded parkas,
let me share with you the finer points of our four seasons. Yes,
there are *four* seasons, not just winter and road construction. And
there's nothing like the beauty of fresh, clean white snow, especially when we don't have to drive in it. But as the snow piles up,
the cold, dark months drag on, and cabin fever begins to set in,
we're convinced winter is here to stay. Miraculously, each year the
snow melts away, and we watch with wonder as the dead brown
earth blossoms into a lush green landscape of new life right before
our eyes. Soon our spring turns into hot, humid summer days, and
we're back to hard work, mosquito slapping, and weekend trips to
the nearest lake. As the autumn leaves begin to fall, we watch the
farmers harvest the fruits of their summer labor while we pull the
dock out of the lake, store the lawn furniture, and get ready for
winter all over again.

Just as God planned the seasons in Minnesota, He designed
four seasons in our lives, each with a distinct purpose. These cycles
of life all work together to nurture our relationship with Christ.
Our winters are often times of hardship or grief. They may mark
an end to a certain life stage or a time when God is calling us
closer to himself to give us comfort and rest. Our springtimes are

filled with the excitement of new adventures and opportunities. During the summers of our lives, we work hard on all that God has given us to do and prepare for the storms that are sure to come our way. At harvest time, we enjoy the fruit of our labor . . . the love, joy, peace, patience, kindness, and other character traits that only come by allowing Christ to control our hearts (Galatians 5:22).

My cancer treatment spanned an entire Minnesota winter. But the end coincided with springtime and all the excitement of a new beginning. With the victory of the risen Christ that Easter morning, I received the precious gift of hope in the future. Even my hair sprouted in perfect time with the spring flowers in my garden! God made everything beautiful in His own time (Ecclesiastes 3:11). In the dead of winter, our finite minds simply can't see or understand the infinite aspects of His nature or His plan for our lives. Right now, you may have a full-blown case of cabin fever . . . the snow is piling up and each day seems colder and darker than the last. Resist the temptation to resent God's perfect timing. It can only lead to despair and hopelessness. Instead, let Him give you comfort and rest during the winter season of your soul. Remember, spring *always* comes . . . even in Minnesota. ❦

GET OUT OF THE BOAT

> ABOUT THREE O'CLOCK IN THE MORNING
> JESUS CAME TO THEM, WALKING ON THE
> WATER. WHEN THE DISCIPLES SAW HIM,
> THEY SCREAMED IN TERROR, THINKING HE
> WAS A GHOST. BUT JESUS SPOKE TO THEM AT
> ONCE. "IT'S ALL RIGHT," HE SAID. "I AM
> HERE! DON'T BE AFRAID." THEN PETER
> CALLED TO HIM, "LORD, IF IT'S REALLY YOU,
> TELL ME TO COME TO YOU BY WALKING ON
> WATER." "ALL RIGHT, COME," JESUS SAID. SO
> PETER WENT OVER THE SIDE OF THE BOAT
> AND WALKED ON THE WATER TOWARD
> JESUS. BUT WHEN HE LOOKED AROUND AT
> THE HIGH WAVES, HE WAS TERRIFIED AND
> BEGAN TO SINK. "SAVE ME, LORD!" HE
> SHOUTED. INSTANTLY JESUS REACHED OUT
> HIS HAND AND GRABBED HIM. "YOU DON'T
> HAVE MUCH FAITH," JESUS SAID. "WHY DID
> YOU DOUBT ME?" AND WHEN THEY CLIMBED
> BACK INTO THE BOAT, THE WIND STOPPED.
> *Matthew 14:25–32*

I know exactly how Peter felt. My eyes were firmly planted on Jesus. There was simply no other way to get through this nightmare, no other option but to trust Him. Where else can you turn when your life is on the line and your back is against the wall? I immersed myself in the Word and prayer until it carried me through every difficult decision, every chemo treatment, and every blood test. I was so filled with faith and wonder at the miracles and promises of God, I'm pretty sure I was walking on water, right into the loving arms of the Lord.

Then it would happen . . . an article in the newspaper, an e-mail from a scientific journal service, or a thoughtless comment from a friend or acquaintance. "Researchers have discovered a promising new treatment for breast cancer." *But I'm not on that drug . . . should I be?* "The survival rate for breast cancer is x%." *Is that all?* "A woman I knew at work died of breast cancer." *Now, that's really helpful to know!* And my favorite, "Well, at least *you* know how you're going to die." *Excuse me?!* Before long, I'm at the bottom of the lake with Peter.

Peter's faith gave him the boldness and courage to step out of the boat and experience God's power. He only started to sink because he took his eyes off Jesus and started focusing on the high waves around him. The same thing can happen to you and me. If we start focusing on our circumstances and take our eyes off the Lord and His promises, we can sink into a state of hopelessness and fear. But like Peter, if we start out with good intentions and our faith falters, it doesn't mean we've failed. Peter was afraid, but he had enough sense to cry out for Christ, the only source of help. Jesus grabbed him, put him safely back into the boat, and stopped the swirling wind around him.

God knows you intimately. He knows when your faith is strong enough to walk on water, and He knows when to pull you up from the bottom of the lake. But He can't help you if you're afraid to leave the boat. Trust Him with all your heart, soul, and mind. You may get wet, but He won't let you drown. ❦

HALLELUJAH ANYWAY!

> EVEN THOUGH THE FIG TREES HAVE NO
> BLOSSOMS, AND THERE ARE NO GRAPES ON
> THE VINE; EVEN THOUGH THE OLIVE CROP
> FAILS, AND THE FIELDS LIE EMPTY AND
> BARREN; EVEN THOUGH THE FLOCKS DIE IN
> THE FIELDS, AND THE CATTLE BARNS ARE
> EMPTY, YET I WILL REJOICE IN THE LORD!
> I WILL BE JOYFUL IN THE GOD
> OF MY SALVATION.
> *Habakkuk 3:17–18*

If only we had our debts paid off . . .

If only we could afford our dream home on the lake . . .

If I can just get my son through high school . . .

If only I had a better boss . . .

If I can just make it through these last rounds of chemo . . .

If only my hair would start growing back . . .

Then I could be happy. How many times have these thoughts gone through your mind—that you are just one event or one situation away from being truly happy? Unfortunately, true happiness does not come when the current problem is resolved because more problems are on the way. When you tie your happiness to circumstances and events you can't control, your life will be a roller coaster of emotional ups and downs.

There is another path to happiness, a path you *can* control. The prophet Habakkuk found it when he looked around at a dying world and rejoiced in the Lord anyway. His feelings were not controlled by barren fields and empty barns but by his faith in God's ability to give him strength. Paul found it when he wrote about being content in every situation, whether extreme poverty, abundant wealth, physical pain, or imprisonment (Philippians 4:11–13). Both Habakkuk and Paul discovered that happiness depends on "happenings," but true joy depends on Christ.

Joy is a precious gift that comes by letting the Holy Spirit control your life (Galatians 5:22). It doesn't depend on your health, your finances, or any other circumstance, but on your relationship with the risen Lord. It comes from knowing He loves you, He lives in you, and He has completely forgiven you of every sin. It comes from an unshakable hope in God's ultimate gift of salvation. Cancer will take you on a wild roller coaster ride with up days, down days, and everything in between. But *you* are a precious child of God. Let His spirit fill you so full that no test result, no side effect, and no amount of uncertainty can steal your joy. When the joy of Christ reigns in your heart, it won't matter what life throws at you. You'll sing hallelujah anyway! 🐾

CLAIM YOUR VICTORY

> FOREVER, O LORD, YOUR WORD STANDS
> FIRM IN HEAVEN. YOUR FAITHFULNESS
> EXTENDS TO EVERY GENERATION, AS
> ENDURING AS THE EARTH YOU CREATED.
> YOUR LAWS REMAIN TRUE TODAY, FOR
> EVERYTHING SERVES YOUR PLANS. IF YOUR
> LAW HADN'T SUSTAINED ME WITH JOY, I
> WOULD HAVE DIED IN MY MISERY. I WILL
> NEVER FORGET YOUR COMMANDMENTS, FOR
> YOU HAVE USED THEM TO RESTORE MY JOY
> AND HEALTH.
> *Psalm 119:89–93*

As I carefully examined my head in the mirror, I was excited to see hundreds of tiny little dark hairs filling in the pores on my scalp. It had been seven months since my husband shaved off what was left of my shedding hair, and I was officially on the other side of my cancer journey. My test results were good and I felt great, but I still had not heard the words "you are healed" from my doctor. The reason, he explained, is that while most women do well, others have a recurrence. Although my prognosis was good, he had no way of knowing what group I'd fall into. So instead, I received resources on how to cope with my uncertain future.

I prayed about how I was going to live the rest of my life under this dark cloud of uncertainty. Gradually, the Lord showed me that I didn't have to settle for a doubtful future and I didn't need the words of my doctor to pronounce my healing. When Thomas said he wouldn't believe in the resurrected Christ until he saw the nail marks in His hands, Jesus said, "Blessed are those *who have not seen and yet have believed*" (John 20:24–30 NIV, emphasis added). To the bleeding woman who believed she would be healed if she only touched His cloak, Jesus said, "your *faith* has healed you" (Matthew 9:20–22 NIV, emphasis added). I prayed for the courage to step out in faith and put my trust in the Word of God. I claimed His healing promises in the name of Jesus Christ.

Often during your cancer journey it will seem like your physical circumstances don't agree with the promises you read in your Bible (John 16:33). But don't let God's Word be limited by the things you see and hear around you. Like all our worldly problems, cancer is temporary and subject to change. But God is the same yesterday, today, and forever (Hebrews 13:8). His Word stands firm in the heavens. He is forever faithful and will *never* abandon you (Hebrews 13:5). His Son proved it when He personally carried away your sin and sickness in His own body on the cross (1 Peter 2:24). Never forget His laws, for He will use them to restore your joy and your health. In faith, make *His* Word your final authority. Instead of settling for an uncertain future, claim the victory Christ has won for you! ❦

Your Secret Weapon

> Then Asa cried out to the Lord his God, "O Lord, no one but you can help the powerless against the mighty! Help us, O Lord our God, for we trust in you alone. It is in your name that we have come against this vast horde. O Lord, you are our God; do not let mere men prevail against you!"
>
> *2 Chronicles 14:11*

The first time my husband and I went hiking in the Canadian Rockies we were clueless. We started up the narrow trail without proper clothing or equipment and found ourselves gasping for breath as our feet slipped over the slippery snow-covered rocks. I remember stopping to rest and feeling as though I couldn't possibly go on. But when I looked down at the steep treacherous trail we had just climbed, I realized there was no turning back either. For a moment, I felt trapped and could see no way of escape.

When life falls apart around us we often resort to our own resources to pick up the pieces and fix the problem. Cancer caught me without an escape plan. Nothing I could do on my own power could change the diagnosis, the treatment, or the outcome. It pushed my back against the wall and left me nowhere to turn, just like that day on the mountain. What do you do when the battles you face seem insurmountable and you see no way out? King Asa had a secret weapon. When he faced an army of a million men, he recognized he was powerless against them and cried out to God for help. He admitted the futility of his own human effort and trusted God to save the people of Judah. The Lord soundly defeated the enemy and handed him the victory (2 Chronicles 14:8–14).

Trusting God is a choice. He can do great and mighty things through us when we recognize our limitations and get out of His way (2 Corinthians 12:9). If this cancer has you trapped on a dangerous one-way mountain trail and you see no escape route, cast all your cares on Jesus (1 Peter 5:7). Let Him carry your load. You may not be able to choose the path you're on and it will probably be a long and hard climb, but you have a secret weapon. . . . and you can trust Him to deliver your victory. ❦

MORE THAN ENOUGH

> I ASSURE YOU, EVEN IF YOU HAD FAITH AS
> SMALL AS A MUSTARD SEED YOU COULD SAY
> TO THIS MOUNTAIN, "MOVE FROM HERE TO
> THERE," AND IT WOULD MOVE. NOTHING
> WOULD BE IMPOSSIBLE.
> *Matthew 17:20*

f I were in your situation, I don't think I would have as much faith as you have." Every time I heard these words I thought, "If you only knew!" Now Abraham had faith. He waited years for the son God promised when he and his wife, Sarah, were old and childless, and then he was willing to sacrifice his son for God. Because Abraham was so faithful, God gave him descendents as numerous as the stars (Genesis 15–22). There were days during my cancer journey when my faith felt as big as Abraham's. Other days it was so small it wouldn't have filled a thimble.

Jesus said that even a tiny amount of faith in God is enough for Him to move your mountain. For a long time this verse confused me. What's wrong with me that I can't muster up even enough faith as a tiny mustard seed, the tiniest particle imaginable? And if I do, is it enough? How much faith do I need before God will hear me and answer my prayers?

Faith is not something we obtain on our own power and it's not always something we see or feel. Like salvation, faith is a *gift* from God (Ephesians 2:8–9). The amount is not nearly as important as having the right kind. There is great power in even a small amount of faith if it's genuine. Just a tiny amount of real faith in

God's power will take you a lot further than a truckload of faith in your own resources.

Don't worry that your faith feels too small to move your mountain. All it takes is a little faith the size of a mustard seed to take root in your heart. Water it daily by renewing your trust in Jesus. Keep asking Him every day for the faith you need to face this cancer. Then trust that whatever He gives you will be more than enough. Before you know it, you'll have faith as big as Abraham's. 🌿

I WANT MY LIFE BACK

> "FOR I KNOW THE PLANS I HAVE FOR YOU,"
> SAYS THE LORD. "THEY ARE PLANS FOR
> GOOD AND NOT FOR DISASTER, TO GIVE YOU
> A FUTURE AND A HOPE. IN THOSE DAYS
> WHEN YOU PRAY, I WILL LISTEN. IF YOU
> LOOK FOR ME IN EARNEST, YOU WILL FIND
> ME WHEN YOU SEEK ME. I WILL BE FOUND BY
> YOU," SAYS THE LORD. "I WILL END YOUR
> CAPTIVITY AND RESTORE YOUR FORTUNES. I
> WILL GATHER YOU OUT OF THE NATIONS
> WHERE I SENT YOU AND BRING YOU HOME
> AGAIN TO YOUR OWN LAND."
> *Jeremiah 29:11–14*

*G*etting ready to go out in public took on a whole new dimension. When I had hair, I used to spend half an hour drying and styling it. Now I spent half an hour drawing eyebrows and eyelashes on my face so I didn't look quite so much like Uncle Fester in the *Addams Family*. I washed my "hair" separately in the sink the night before, let it dry on a wig stand, and fluffed it with my fingers before I plopped it on my head in the morning. Instead of fretting over a bad hair day or lousy hair cut, I now worried my hair would slip out of place or worse, blow off my head. One day a stranger in church complimented me on my hair and asked me where I had it styled. I almost pulled it off my head and handed it to her. *You want it? You can have it. I want my life back.*

I wonder if the people of Judah felt the same way when they were in exile. God brought their ancestors to the Promised Land

and blessed them with freedom and prosperity. But they continually turned away from God and fell into sin. After a history of repentance and delivery, Jerusalem was eventually destroyed and the people were captured and carried off to Babylon. Even then, God didn't forget them. He sent a message of hope through the prophet Jeremiah and in time brought them back to their homeland with renewed hearts for God.

The Lord did not forget the people of Judah, He didn't forget me, and He won't forget you. You have His awesome presence and His amazing grace. If you turn to Him in prayer, He will listen. If you seek Him with all your heart, you will find Him. He wants to give you a new beginning, a new purpose, and renewed hope in the future. He wants to end your captivity and restore your prosperity. He wants to give your life back . . . and He wants to be in the center. ❧

His Grace is All You Need

> Each time he said, "My gracious favor
> is all you need. My power works best
> in your weakness." So now I am glad to
> boast about my weaknesses, so that the
> power of Christ may work through
> me. Since I know it is all for Christ's
> good, I am quite content with my
> weaknesses and with insults, hardships,
> persecutions, and calamities. For when
> I am weak, then I am strong.
> *2 Corinthians 12:9–10*

The apostle Paul was always a high achiever, even before his conversion on the road to Damascus (Acts 9:1–19). After God re-focused his fierce passion from persecuting Christians to preaching Christ, he spread the gospel message throughout the Roman Empire. The letters he wrote to the churches became part of the New Testament. At some point during this time, Paul was afflicted with a thorn in his flesh that was thought to be some sort of physical ailment. He asked the Lord to remove it three times, and three times the Lord said, "No, my grace is all you need, my power works best in your weakness." He went on to do even greater things in spite of this affliction, because the thorn forced him to rely on God instead of his own abilities and resources.

For the first half of my life I worked very hard at serving and pleasing God and everyone else on my own power. I could deliver a perfect talk, lead a perfect meeting, serve a perfect holiday dinner, and keep all the balls in the air at once, without giving much thought to asking God for help. Then came cancer. All my knowledge and abilities, everything I knew, everything I leaned on, everything I trusted, was stripped away. I couldn't even trust my own body. All I could do was trust God. He healed my cancer, but He left the thorn. The mark it made deep within my soul keeps me on my knees. It is a constant reminder that Jesus is all I need. It keeps me humble and focused on Him. It is in this place of weakness where His power works best.

It's our human nature not to trust Christ when we think we are strong and competent. But when everything in your world is stripped away, is He enough? When cancer tries to steal your health, your self-esteem, and your hope, is He enough? Paul found out He was more than enough. Wherever you are in your cancer journey, the power of Christ works best in your weakness. Trust Him today, and He will give you all the strength you need (Philippians 4:13). Trust Him tomorrow, and He can accomplish more than you would dare ask or hope (Ephesians 3:20). For when you are weak, then He is strong. His grace is all you need. ❧

WHO IS THIS JESUS?

> WHEN JESUS CAME TO THE REGION OF
> CAESAREA PHILIPPI, HE ASKED HIS DISCIPLES,
> "WHO DO PEOPLE SAY THAT THE SON OF
> MAN IS?" "WELL," THEY REPLIED, "SOME SAY
> JOHN THE BAPTIST, SOME SAY ELIJAH, AND
> OTHERS SAY JEREMIAH OR ONE OF THE
> OTHER PROPHETS." THEN HE ASKED THEM,
> "WHO DO YOU SAY I AM?"
> *Matthew 16: 13–15*

f Jesus asked you this question today, how would you answer?
Was He simply a prominent historical figure, a Jewish teacher
who was brutally crucified on a cross? Perhaps one of the great
prophets come back to life? Or is He the Christ, the Lamb of
God, His eternal Son sent to earth as a man to die for the sins of
all humankind?

Simon Peter answered this question by calling Jesus the Messiah, the Son of the living God. Jesus blessed this first confession
of faith by making Peter the first great leader in the church at
Jerusalem and handing him the keys to the kingdom of heaven
(Matthew 16:17–19). The Bible promises those who follow in
Peter's footsteps and confess that Jesus is Lord can have:

- Faith instead of fear (John 6:18–19)
- Health instead of sickness (Psalm 30:2)
- Hope instead of despair (Jeremiah 29:11)
- Peace instead of worry (Philippians 4:6–7)
- Provision instead of lack (Philippians 4:19)

Just imagine for a moment. In the midst of our suffering, we can have a quality of life that knows no anxiety, no doubt, and no hopelessness. . . . a quality of life where no test report, no doctor visit, and no chemo treatment can penetrate the perfect peace that rests deep within our spirit.

Do you hunger for peace like this? Have you invited Jesus into the center of your cancer? You should know the Lord is a gentleman. He will not come barging uninvited through your front door like a knight in shining armor, claiming to be your Messiah and demanding that you surrender your life to Him. You are not a puppet on a string, and He is not some divine puppeteer orchestrating your every thought and every move from the heavenly realm. He chose you first, to love you and die for you, to invite you into His kingdom to live with Him forever (John 15:16). But He gave you the freedom to accept or reject His offer. Who is this Jesus? The final choice is yours. Choose wisely . . . your very life depends on it. 🌿

A THOUSAND MAY FALL

> THOSE WHO LIVE IN THE SHELTER OF THE
> MOST HIGH WILL FIND REST IN THE SHADOW
> OF THE ALMIGHTY. THIS I DECLARE OF THE
> LORD: HE ALONE IS MY REFUGE, MY PLACE
> OF SAFETY; HE IS MY GOD, AND I AM
> TRUSTING HIM. FOR HE WILL RESCUE YOU
> FROM EVERY TRAP AND PROTECT YOU
> FROM THE FATAL PLAGUE. HE WILL SHIELD
> YOU WITH HIS WINGS. HE WILL SHELTER
> YOU WITH HIS FEATHERS. HIS FAITHFUL
> PROMISES ARE YOUR ARMOR AND
> PROTECTION. DO NOT BE AFRAID OF THE
> TERRORS OF THE NIGHT, NOR FEAR THE
> DANGERS OF THE DAY, NOR DREAD THE
> PLAGUE THAT STALKS IN DARKNESS, NOR THE
> DISASTER THAT STRIKES AT MIDDAY.
> THOUGH A THOUSAND FALL AT YOUR SIDE,
> THOUGH TEN THOUSAND ARE DYING
> AROUND YOU, THESE EVILS WILL NOT
> TOUCH YOU.
> *Psalm 91:1–7*

Psalm 91 is a powerful promise of God's protection. If you make the Lord your dwelling place, if you seek rest within His shadow, if you abide in Him and trust Him with all your heart, He promises to protect you from every trap and every fatal disease the devil sends your way. As I lay in bed the nights my body ached after chemo treatments, I visualized myself in this secret place, huddled under the shelter of His wings. I was protected from any harm these powerful drugs might do to my healthy cells and hidden from any threat this plague might pose to the rest of my body. I visualized the evils of cancer not touching me, even though thousands fell on both sides.

But Lord, that's not fair! It's not fair that anyone should fall at my right or my left! I know some of the fallen and they were good people. And why should they fall, while I stand protected under the shelter of your wings? And because I couldn't settle the conflict in my limited, finite mind, I started doubting the promise . . . and before too long, I started doubting the One who made it.

Peter had the same thoughts. After His resurrection, Jesus let Peter know the kind of death he would die to glorify God. He responded by asking about John, the disciple Jesus loved, "What about him, Lord?" Jesus replied, "If I want him to remain alive until I return, what is that to you? You follow me" (John 21:18–23). Jesus essentially told Peter it was none of his business what became of John. No matter what Peter's future held, the Lord told him to follow Him.

Our human tendency is to compare our lives with others, either to rationalize our own level of faithfulness and devotion or to question God's justice. But God is sovereign. His ways are higher than ours, and His thoughts are higher than ours (Isaiah 55:8–9). If we start making our human understanding of justice and fairness a condition for our faith in Him, we have no faith at all. God is God, and we're not.

As you meditate on His Word today, know that this psalm was written just for you. This promise is between you and God. Resist the temptation to try to figure out what it means for others. The Lord said it's none of your business. He wants your total surrender, your total trust, and that includes surrendering the need to know. Don't let your failure to understand all the ways of your Creator rob you of your armor and protection. Open up your heart and receive His promise: a thousand may fall at your right, and ten thousand at your left, and these evils will not touch you. ❦

THIS IS WHAT THE LORD SAYS: DO NOT BE
AFRAID! DON'T BE DISCOURAGED BY THIS
MIGHTY ARMY, FOR THE BATTLE IS NOT
YOURS, BUT GOD'S . . . AFTER CONSULTING
THE LEADERS OF THE PEOPLE, THE KING
APPOINTED SINGERS TO WALK AHEAD OF THE
ARMY, SINGING TO THE LORD AND PRAISING
HIM FOR HIS HOLY SPLENDOR. THIS IS WHAT
THEY SANG: "GIVE THANKS TO THE LORD;
HIS FAITHFUL LOVE ENDURES FOREVER!" AT
THE MOMENT THEY BEGAN TO SING AND
GIVE PRAISE, THE LORD CAUSED THE ARMIES
OF AMMON, MOAB, AND MOUNT SEIR TO
START FIGHTING AMONG THEMSELVES. . . .
THERE WAS SO MUCH PLUNDER THAT IT
TOOK THEM THREE DAYS JUST TO COLLECT
IT ALL! ON THE FOURTH DAY THEY
GATHERED IN THE VALLEY OF BLESSING,
WHICH GOT ITS NAME THAT DAY BECAUSE
THE PEOPLE PRAISED AND THANKED THE
LORD THERE.

2 Chronicles 20:15, 21–23, 25–26

When King Jehoshaphat heard that a vast army of Moabites, Ammonites, and Menuites were mounting an attack against him, he cried out for God to rescue the people. As the mighty army approached, God sent word that the people should not be afraid, for the battle was not theirs but God's. He promised they would not even need to fight! The next day, the king appointed singers to walk ahead of the army to sing and give praise to the Lord. At the sound of their voices, the Lord set the enemy armies into confusion and they fought against one another. Not a single one escaped, and not a single Israelite was killed. There was so much equipment, clothing, and other valuables it took the people three days to collect all the plunder. Finally, on the fourth day, they gathered in the Valley of Blessing to praise and thank the Lord for their victory.

Imagine how much faith and obedience it took for King Jehoshaphat to march into battle with a band of praise singers leading the charge instead of a band of warriors. When the doctor confirmed my breast cancer and explained the battle ahead of me, singing praises to the Lord was not first and foremost on my mind! Beating my cancer with every medical weapon in the arsenal seemed like a much better battle plan.

My cancer felt like a mighty army marching against me. The chemo and the radiation offered hope, but no guarantee of victory. When I cried out to the Lord to rescue me and gave Him control of my cancer, I made it His battle, not mine. I didn't have an army of musicians to send ahead, but I could praise Him and thank Him for all my blessings. And I did have Christian radio. I played it all day and all night. It filled my house with wonderful praise music and teaching from God's Word. On the difficult days, I let it soak into me like a soothing balm until His unwavering promises became etched on my heart.

Are you looking for victory today? Then turn on your radio, go find a Spirit-filled worship service, and shout your praises to the Lord! The battle against your cancer does not belong to you; it doesn't even belong to your doctors. It belongs to God. It may have formed an army against you, but His Son already defeated it for you at the Cross. You don't have to wait until the battle is over to start celebrating. Send your praises on ahead and soon that deep valley of suffering, the battlefield of your cancer, will become your Valley of Blessing. And it will take years to haul your blessings home. ❦

JUST FOR YOU

> HE WAS DESPISED AND REJECTED—A MAN OF
> SORROWS, ACQUAINTED WITH BITTEREST
> GRIEF. WE TURNED OUR BACKS ON HIM AND
> LOOKED THE OTHER WAY WHEN HE WENT
> BY. HE WAS DESPISED, AND WE DID NOT
> CARE. YET IT WAS OUR SICKNESSES HE
> CARRIED; IT WAS OUR DISEASES THAT
> WEIGHED HIM DOWN. AND WE THOUGHT HIS
> TROUBLES WERE A PUNISHMENT FROM GOD
> FOR HIS OWN SINS! BUT HE WAS WOUNDED
> AND CRUSHED FOR OUR SINS. HE WAS
> BEATEN THAT WE MIGHT HAVE PEACE. HE
> WAS WHIPPED, AND WE WERE HEALED!
> *Isaiah 53:3–5*

His name is Jesus. Over three hundred prophesies in the Old Testament predicted He would come to save you. He existed in the very beginning. He was with God, He was God, and He created all things (John 1:1–3). He merely spoke and the foundation of the earth was laid, the moon and stars were set in the heavens, and the sea and lands were filled with plants and creatures. And then, because He loved you so much, He orchestrated the perfect plan to redeem you from the sin that had come into the world through one man (Romans 5:12). He became human. When He walked the earth as a man, He healed the sick, fulfilling the word of the prophet Isaiah, who said, "He took our sicknesses and removed our diseases" (Matthew 8:16–17). And then He died on a cross.

For years, I would go to our Good Friday church service and watch Frank, our janitor turned Jesus, drag the cross up the center aisle. I would cringe when the men dressed like Roman soldiers "pounded" the nails into his hands and feet. The spring of my cancer, after I had finished eight rounds of chemo and was halfway through radiation treatment, I watched this Good Friday scene unfold once again. This time, when the nails were driven into Frank's hands, I sobbed. This time, it was personal. I taped a nail to the front of my computer monitor that night and it has been there ever since. I don't ever want to forget the price He paid. I don't ever want to forget how He suffered and died in my place. The nail is a constant reminder of His love for me.

His name is Jesus. He has power and authority over sin—over all evil powers and earthly disease. When they whipped Him, you were healed. When He dragged the cross up the hill to Calvary, He carried the weight of your cancer on His back. When they nailed Him to the cross, He defeated your cancer and carried it with Him to the grave. He died to save us all, but He would have done it just for you. ❦

DRUGSTORE JESUS

> AND I AM SURE THAT GOD, WHO BEGAN
> THE GOOD WORK WITHIN YOU, WILL
> CONTINUE HIS WORK UNTIL IT IS FINALLY
> FINISHED ON THAT DAY WHEN CHRIST JESUS
> COMES BACK AGAIN.
> *Philippians 1:6*

It was no longer enough for Him to be the one-hour God of my Sunday mornings or the quick-fix "drugstore Jesus" I turned to in times of crisis. Cancer was just too big for an occasional dose of religion or a weekly spiritual pep talk. It consumed my thoughts, it consumed my time, and for several months, it consumed my life. When I invited Him into the center of it, He took charge. He took charge of the surgeon's hands and every treatment decision. He took charge when the nurses couldn't find one more vein to administer the chemo. He took charge of the side effects, and He took charge of my family. He took charge of my clients when I didn't feel like talking. He took charge the first time I had to go out in public without hair. By the time it was all over, He had taken charge of my heart.

When the chemo is finished, the fatigue is lifted, your hair grows back, and your hope returns, you may be tempted to slip back into your old life. In fact, you may long for it! But things will never be the same again. From the moment you cried out to the Lord and gave Him authority over your cancer, He began to mold you and shape you into the masterpiece He created. He is preparing you to do the good things He planned for you long ago (Ephesians 2:8–10). Through the power of the Holy Spirit living within you, He wants to transform you from the inside out and draw you closer and closer to the very heart of Christ. He wants your roots to go down deep into the soil of His love so you can fully experience all He has to offer . . . a fullness of life that only comes from God . . . a fullness of life that goes way beyond your cancer (Ephesians 3:17–19).

Be careful to stand firm and not drift away from the gift He gave when you needed it most (Colossians 1:23). He is not some drugstore Jesus, like aspirin sitting forgotten on the shelf until you need it to relieve your current pain, and then left alone until your next headache. He wants to finish the work He started when you first called out for Him to save you. He wants to be more than the Lord of your cancer. He wants to be the Lord of your life. ❦

HE HEARS YOU KNOCKING

> AND SO I TELL YOU, KEEP ON ASKING, AND
> YOU WILL BE GIVEN WHAT YOU ASK FOR.
> KEEP ON LOOKING, AND YOU WILL FIND.
> KEEP ON KNOCKING, AND THE DOOR WILL
> BE OPENED. FOR EVERYONE WHO ASKS,
> RECEIVES. EVERYONE WHO SEEKS, FINDS.
> AND THE DOOR IS OPENED TO EVERYONE
> WHO KNOCKS.
> *Luke 11:9–10*

Before breast cancer, my prayer life was limited to the prayers spoken at church and an occasional prayer before meals and bedtime. When I did pray, my prayers were often more like shopping lists than actual conversations with God. Sometimes I would put together some elaborate plan without consulting Him at all and then pray that He would bless it. I usually saved my serious praying for the big stuff, assuming God didn't want to be bothered with the daily details. When we pray, we often ask for the wrong things, ask with the wrong motives, or we don't ask at all. And then we wonder why He's silent (James 4:2–3).

Jesus taught us to praise God *first*, then ask (Luke 11:1–4). In the beginning, it was hard to pray at all, let alone to praise God first. When I felt sick or tired, or discouraged about the journey ahead of me, the only thing I wanted to ask was for Him to make it all go away. I gradually learned that surrendering to God in prayer helped me connect directly into His blessing and power. As I developed a regular prayer life, I became more and more dependent on Him. Eventually, it became natural to praise Him and ask

77

for *everything* I needed. Amazing things happened. A prayer for relief from side effects would result in a peaceful night of rest. A prayer for companionship would result in a phone call from my brother or a friend. A prayer for groceries would result in a surprise dinner out with my husband. The more I asked, the more I received. The more I sought Him, the more I found Him.

How is your prayer life? Perhaps you've been standing outside in the cold too long. All you need is a humble heart and sincere faith to seek God in prayer. Give *praise* because He is an awesome God; *confess* your brokenness and your need for Him; *ask* because He is the giver of all good things. Pray to the Father, in the name of His Son, in the power of the Spirit. Ask God to change your desires so they line up perfectly with His will (1 John 3:21–22). Ask and expect to receive. He hears you knocking, and He always opens the door. ❧

UNLEASH THE POWER

> ARE ANY AMONG YOU SICK? THEY SHOULD
> CALL FOR THE ELDERS OF THE CHURCH AND
> HAVE THEM PRAY OVER THEM, ANOINTING
> THEM WITH OIL IN THE NAME OF THE LORD.
> AND THEIR PRAYER OFFERED IN FAITH WILL
> HEAL THE SICK, AND THE LORD WILL MAKE
> THEM WELL. AND ANYONE WHO HAS
> COMMITTED SINS WILL BE FORGIVEN.
> *James 5:14–15*

We were hardwired to communicate with God through prayer. When we are sick and afraid and our heart is breaking and our inward spirit aches for His physical presence, it's the only way to reach out and touch Him. We hunger for it. We seek it in our churches; we seek it among our Christian friends. Jesus promised when two or three are gathered in His name and agree on what they ask, He is in the midst of them and His Father in heaven will do what they ask (Matthew 18:20). All too often, instead of gathering around and praying over us as the Word commands, friends quietly tell us we're *in* their prayers. And at church, our prayer requests often slip discreetly into the hands of strangers on a prayer chain. It's just more comfortable that way . . . no less effective, just more comfortable.

I've seen the knees of the mightiest prayer warriors weaken at the thought of praying aloud in a circle of corporate prayer. Some think only pastors and priests are qualified. Many simply believe prayer is a private matter. If this has been your experience, you could be missing out on something powerful. Shortly after my diagnosis, after I had come to terms with the seriousness of my cancer and my total helplessness against it, I turned to my local church home. Several prayer ministers surrounded me, gently laying their hands on my shoulders, and prayed for my healing. These people were not pastors but lay people like you and me. They were acting in total obedience to the Word of God. They were so in tune with the Holy Spirit that the words they prayed spoke directly into the deepest unspoken fears in my heart. God was in the center of the circle. When they touched me, He touched me. When they anointed my head with oil, He anointed my head with oil. When they wiped away my tears, He wiped away my tears. I had never felt so close to the very heart and mind of Christ. I had never felt so loved. And at that moment I knew my cancer was in His hands . . . not mine, not the doctors, only His.

Now that I'm on the other side of breast cancer, I am a part of this circle, this time as one who has walked the path before. God has placed His servants everywhere, people who want to pray with you and give you the same comfort He gave them in times of their deepest trouble (2 Corinthians 1:3–4). Seek them out. If you can't find them in your local church, ask God to help you find them. Call on them to pray over you in the name of the Lord. Their prayers will unleash power like you've never seen before. ❦

May I Have Your Attention Please?

> WHO ARE YOU, A MERE HUMAN BEING, TO
> CRITICIZE GOD? SHOULD THE THING THAT
> WAS CREATED SAY TO THE ONE WHO MADE
> IT, "WHY HAVE YOU MADE ME LIKE THIS?"
> WHEN A POTTER MAKES JARS OUT OF CLAY,
> DOESN'T HE HAVE A RIGHT TO USE THE SAME
> LUMP OF CLAY TO MAKE ONE JAR FOR
> DECORATION AND ANOTHER TO
> THROW GARBAGE INTO?
> *Romans 9:20–21*

Somewhere along the line, I got confused. Maybe it started when I was burning my bra and singing, "I am woman, hear me roar." Maybe it happened before then. At some point, it became all about me. I became the center of my universe. All the important components of my life revolved around me like little planets: family, career, spirituality, health, and community. I deserved to be happy, balanced, and in control of it all. I could buy all kinds of self-improvement books to help me get there, books on how to gain control of my schedule, how to gain control of my body, how to gain control of my family, and how to gain control of my boss. Somehow, through the process of getting *in* balance, I lost my balance.

Maybe that's why breast cancer took me by such surprise. *I have what? That's impossible. . . . I've taken control of my life and I don't have breast cancer on the calendar!* Somewhere in the process of shaping and molding everything else, I thought I could shape and mold God. I had Him conveniently slotted into the "spiritual" compartment of my busy life and called on Him to meet my needs according to my schedule. God will not be shaped or molded like clay. He *is* the potter, and the little pot has no right to demand anything from the one who made it. In fact, if it weren't for the potter, there would be no pot!

When the doctor called that day with the bad news, God got my attention. Each time I looked at my bald head in the mirror, He nudged me further off center. By the time my treatment was over, He had taken His rightful place in the center of my life. He became the potter again, and I became the clay . . . soft, pliable, moldable clay. Clay in the palm of His hand.

Are you prepared to let God be God? Like the potter molding the clay, He knows everything about you (Psalm 139). You can hide no flaw or no defect. Be still and willing to learn from this cancer. Be receptive to what the potter wants to teach you. As you begin yielding to Him, He'll start shaping you into the beautiful vessel He created you to be (Jeremiah 18:6). And He'll do a much better job than any self-improvement book could. Now that He's got your attention, let Him mold you. After all, He did it once before. 🌸

ONLY GOD

> ONLY BY YOUR POWER CAN WE PUSH BACK
> OUR ENEMIES; ONLY IN YOUR NAME CAN WE
> TRAMPLE OUR FOES. I DO NOT TRUST MY
> BOW; I DO NOT COUNT ON MY SWORD TO
> SAVE ME. IT IS YOU WHO GIVES US VICTORY
> OVER OUR ENEMIES.
>
> *Psalm 44:5–7*

The healing coach called it CAM—short for "complementary and alternative medicine." The list she gave me offered a broad range of creative healing approaches for breast cancer that I could use in addition to or in place of my standard medical treatment. I could participate in dance movement therapy or learn to embroider healing talisman symbols or make a healing drum. I could benefit from breathing, imagery, relaxation, yoga, foot massage, reflexology, herbs, acupuncture, dream consultation, Qigong, Reiki, Ayurvedic medicine, and various flower remedies. I was invited to awaken my ancient self through cross-dimensional healing and heal myself through various approaches to mind and body control. I even had the opportunity to meet my "power animals" through Shamanic journeying. I decided to stick with the Lord as my comforter and healer. And He wasn't even on the list.

It can be confusing to evaluate these healing techniques or any new philosophies through the eyes of the world. If our hearts are hardened and we are blind and deaf to the things of God, we cannot turn to Him for healing (Matthew 13:15). Without spiritual eyes and ears, we are easily led astray. But when we accept Christ as Lord and Savior, the Holy Spirit begins to soften our hearts and gives us spiritual eyes so we can recognize His presence in the activity around us. Prayer and staying in the Word keeps our senses sharp so we can hear the voice of God and discern His truth in all the confusion.

As you consider your healing choices today, know this: The Lord is the one who heals your diseases (Exodus 15:25–26; Psalm 103:3). *Everything* else is complementary. He may heal you medically, He may heal you miraculously, He may heal you in the heavenly realm. He may use unexpected methods to help you draw closer to Him. But He alone is the one who heals . . . nothing you do yourself, no drum, no symbols, no doctor. Only God. ❦

THE INNER CIRCLE

YES, EVERYTHING ELSE IS WORTHLESS WHEN
COMPARED WITH THE PRICELESS GAIN OF
KNOWING CHRIST JESUS MY LORD.
Philippians 3:8

You know the president of the United States. You probably know him better than you'd like. You know where he goes on weekends, who his friends are, and when he takes a vacation. You know what he eats for dinner, what vegetables he hates, and the names of his pets. You know his exercise habits, his heart rate, the results of his blood tests, and where he goes to church. You know his views on the world and whether you like him or not. Do you know him well enough to call him on the phone, ask him for help, or just hang out and talk like old friends? Probably not. Unless you are part of his inner circle, he is unlikely to be your personal friend and confidant. You know him well, yet you don't know him at all.

Before my diagnosis, my relationship with the Lord was a little bit like my relationship with the president. I knew all about Him in my head, but we didn't have much happening on a personal level. Then breast cancer came crashing into my life. There were too many options, too few answers, and no guarantees. I knew the Bible said God could take away my fear and anxiety and heal all my diseases, but I needed desperately to experience it. So I decided to get to know Him better. I started reading my Bible every day and spending more time in prayer. Eventually my head knowledge moved down twelve inches. As Jesus became more and more at home in my heart, I started to *experience* His power. And before long, He was my best friend.

In Old Testament times, only temple priests could enter God's presence behind the curtain in the most Holy Place. But first, they had to purify themselves and offer sacrifices according to the Law of Moses. All that changed at Calvary. When Jesus died, the curtain was torn (Luke 23:45). Now, all who confess Jesus is Lord and invite Him into their hearts can come into the presence of God (Romans 10:9). To receive this precious gift is to know Him personally (John 17:3). Don't assume because you haven't experienced His presence and power in your battle with cancer that it doesn't exist or He's out of your reach. Christ died so you could be part of His inner circle. Give Him a call . . . He's anxious to spend some time with you. ❦

DAUGHTER OF THE KING

SO LET US COME BOLDLY TO THE THRONE
OF OUR GRACIOUS GOD. THERE WE WILL
RECEIVE HIS MERCY, AND WE WILL FIND
GRACE TO HELP US WHEN WE NEED IT.
Hebrews 4:16

No one rolled out a red carpet for me and treated me like royalty. I didn't have a personal assistant, a driver, a cook, or servants at my beck and call. I was still a wife and a mom. I had work to do, meals to prepare, and school functions to attend. I tried hard to keep things normal for my family. Some days, I didn't feel normal. My joints ached and my fingers were numb. I got tired of living inside my bald body and driving back and forth to the doctor to be stuck with more needles. In spite of my weariness, there was an underlying peace . . . a powerful feeling of incredible love . . . a blessed assurance of protection. After all, I *am* the daughter of a King.

It's true. When I accepted Christ as my Savior, I became a child of the Almighty God (Galatians 3:26). As soon as He adopted me into His family, He sent His Son into my heart and told me I could call Him my Father (Galatians 4:6). If that wasn't enough, He gave me *everything* that belongs to Him (Galatians 4:7)! Just imagine—as a true child of Abraham I am entitled to the same blessings God promised him (Galatians 3:29). An abundance of good things, wherever I go and in everything I do . . . blessing upon blessing (Deuteronomy 28:1–13)!

Dear sister, this same Father who took care of me will take care of you. There is plenty in His heavenly treasury for all His children. His glorious riches are more than enough to supply your every need (Philippians 4:19). Your family, your finances, your health, your cancer, whatever your need, your Father can provide. When your enemies attack, your Father who commands all the armies in heaven will conquer and scatter them in seven directions (Deuteronomy 28:7). When people see He has claimed you as His very own child, they will stand in awe of you (Deuteronomy 28:10). When you need to talk to Him, you can go boldly into the throne room and crawl up on your Daddy's lap. After all, you are His child, a princess of the Almighty God . . . you're the daughter of the King. 🌸

LOVE LETTER FROM HEAVEN

THE GRASS WITHERS, AND THE FLOWERS
FADE, BUT THE WORD OF OUR GOD
STANDS FOREVER.
Isaiah 40:8

The most beautiful book ever written stood forgotten on a shelf collecting dust. For weeks, I desperately searched medical self-help books and Internet articles for evidence that this subtle thickening in my left breast couldn't possibly be cancer. *How could it be?* I had no family history. I must have touched the area a hundred times a day. Maybe this time it would be gone. It doesn't really *feel* like the lump described in the book. It doesn't feel at all like the little pea-sized lump in the breast model they use to teach breast self-exams. Even my doctor was skeptical at first. *What else could it possibly be?* Some kind of cyst or just an innocent lump of breast tissue perhaps? With each test came more suspicion and the need for more tests. My mind was a battlefield and I was losing the battle. The day before hearing the final biopsy results I finally reached for the Book.

I was not in the habit of reading the Bible much on my own. I was not sure where to go or what I was looking for, but I always loved Psalm 91. So that's where I started. Over the next months I discovered that the psalms captured every single emotion I encountered during my breast cancer, from the fear and hopelessness in the beginning to the Lord's glorious victory in the end. I immersed myself in this beautiful, powerful book of poetry and let the Word of God wash over me like a gentle rain.

Whether daily Bible reading is new to you or you've been in the habit for years, curl up in a comfy chair and get ready for a treat. The book of Psalms is sure to capture your every thought, your every hurt, your secret longings, and your deepest prayers. Each day, King David and the other authors will take you on a journey into the very heart and soul of your cancer. Their beautiful words will describe:

- The tears you cry into your pillow at night (6, 69)
- The fears you face each day (34, 40, 46)
- Your cries to the Lord for help (17, 31, 57)
- Your despair when He seems far away (10, 22)
- Your place of shelter and refuge (27, 61, 91)
- Your heavenly Father battling your cancer (18, 140, 144)
- His promise of victory (37, 84, 103)
- His unfailing love for you (136, 139)
- Your joy and gratitude when the enemy is defeated (9, 30, 100)

Once you've had a taste of the Word of God, you won't stop with the psalms. You'll discover the most beautiful words ever written. Words that stand the test of time . . . words that reign forever. What else would you expect from a love letter sent directly from heaven?

SET IN STONE

I AM THE LORD, AND I DO NOT CHANGE.
Malachi 3:6

It wasn't like having pneumonia. They couldn't just give me a prescription for an antibiotic and send me to bed for a few weeks. I needed a doctorate degree to understand all the options. Lumpectomy with radiation, mastectomy without radiation, or mastectomy with radiation? *It depends.* Mastectomy with reconstruction? Delayed or immediate? Implant or TRAM flap? *It depends.* Node dissection or sentinel node biopsy, or both? *It depends.* Chemo or no chemo, and if I do chemo, which chemo? *It depends.* Two- or three-week regimen? Should I enroll in a clinical trial? *It depends.* It all depends on what? What this doctor recommends? What that doctor recommends? What my husband thinks? What my family thinks? What my friend who had breast cancer thinks? What I think? *What if I'm wrong?*

What if everyone else is wrong? I was drowning in information. Too many details, too many options, and too few guarantees. Each time I came up for air and started feeling comfortable with my decisions, a new study was released or a new drug was approved or someone would have a different opinion. It was like shooting at a moving target. And why should I be surprised? Thirty years ago doctors weren't even using chemo for breast cancer. Three hundred years ago they were probably using leeches.

You may be blessed with the most brilliant minds in the medical profession to treat your cancer. But science will advance and human opinion will change with the times. What a comfort to know your God never changes! He alone is your rock. When you stand on Him, you will never be shaken (Psalm 62:2). In the midst of all the complexity, you can trust the One who makes it simple. When the world is shifting all around you, you can trust the One who never moves. He is the ultimate physician. He is the same yesterday, today, and forever (Hebrews 13:8). And His treatment plan is set in stone. ❦

BIKER CHICK

BUT WHENEVER ANYONE TURNS TO THE
LORD, THEN THE VEIL IS TAKEN AWAY.
NOW, THE LORD IS THE SPIRIT, AND
WHEREVER THE SPIRIT OF THE LORD IS,
HE GIVES FREEDOM.
2 Corinthians 3:16–17

It's true. I'm a biker chick. My husband and I share a beautiful 2003 GL1800 Gold Wing. Silver . . . with lots and lots of chrome. We belong to a biker ministry group with more than one hundred people who love Jesus, love each other, and love to ride. On Sunday afternoons, the sight and sound of sixty bikes stretched out over miles of country highway is a wonder to behold. When four couples took our Gold Wings on a 5,600-mile cross-country trip recently, I don't know what I enjoyed most—the sheer beauty of His creation, the awesome privilege of showing His love to the people He put in our path, or the fellowship we shared with each other. No human being deserves this much fun.

It wasn't always this way. Before my cancer, I wouldn't have considered joining my husband on a Sunday motorcycle ride with "those people." After all, they were leather-clad, tattooed, head banded, downright scary-looking folks. What would my friends think? What would my clients think? *What would my parents think?* I eventually learned that a veil of pride and hardness of heart blinded me from understanding the love of Christ and the true nature of God. When my cancer journey drew me closer to the Lord and my relationship with Him became personal, the veil was stripped away. God removed the heavy burden of trying to please

Him on my own and all the guilt that comes with it. He removed my pride and my judging spirit and let me see people through His eyes. By accepting His Son into my heart, I am loved, forgiven, accepted, and free! And I'm having the time of my life. I'm leather-clad and downright scary looking.

If you let it, your cancer can unlock the door to the abundant life God always wanted for you (John 10:10). As the Lord becomes more and more at home in your heart, the Holy Spirit will start revealing everything He had planned for you from the very beginning. God knows every burden, everything that binds you, and every lie that holds you captive to the thoughts of this world. He wants to set you free! When you accept His offer of redemption, His overflowing love and forgiveness will remove the stain of your sin and make you clean as freshly fallen snow (Isaiah 1:18). He'll transform you into the child He created. And He'll take you places you never dreamed. Who knows? It might be on a Harley. 🗝

Nothing to Fear

God is our refuge and strength,
always ready to help in times of
trouble. So we will not fear, even if
earthquakes come and the mountains
crumble into the sea. Let the oceans
roar and foam. Let the mountains
tremble as the waters surge!

Psalm 46:1–3

Every once in a while it tries to gain a foothold. It rears its ugly head before a routine checkup or if I have an unexplained headache or backache. It started making an appearance at the very beginning, when my doctor found the lump. When the ultrasound didn't rule out breast cancer, and the possibility became more real, it started escalating. Finally it consumed me. The doctor who performed my needle core biopsy had a less than tactful bedside manner. He was abrupt, unfeeling, and took away whatever hope I had left. By the time I left his office, it had wrapped itself around my throat and suffocated me. My heart raced, my chest tightened, and there was a sick feeling deep in the pit of my stomach. Fear. It had me in a choke hold.

When David fled for his life and hid from Saul in the cave of Adullam, I'm sure he felt the same way. He lost hope and was paralyzed with fear (Psalm 143:4). When he was unable to pull himself out of his deepest despair, he cried out to the Lord in prayer (143:7). David trusted the light of the Lord to conquer the darkness of fear (Psalm 27:1–3). When fear started choking me, I let it take control. I had stopped trusting God. David reminded me I could turn to the Lord in prayer and trust His perfect love to drive fear out before it gained a foothold (1 John 4:18). I wear a necklace engraved with Joshua 1:9 as a constant reminder to cast my fears on Jesus, the one who never leaves my side: "Be strong and courageous! Do not be afraid or discouraged. For the Lord your God is with you wherever you go."

Fear is not from God (2 Timothy 1:7). He knew it would try to gain a foothold in your life, so He gave you a perfect weapon against it. His name is Jesus. His supernatural peace will come upon you when you resist all your worries and bring everything to God in prayer (Philippians 4:6). The peace of Christ is your weapon against all fear. It is not found in positive thinking or a good lab report. It comes only from trusting God. It comes from knowing He alone controls your cancer, your family, your doctors, and your future. When fear tries to hold you prisoner today, will you let it control you or will you be like David? Cry out to the Lord in prayer! Earthquakes may come and mountains may crumble into the sea, but you have nothing to fear. ❦

COATS OF PRIDE

> "GOD SETS HIMSELF AGAINST THE PROUD,
> BUT HE SHOWS FAVOR TO THE HUMBLE." SO
> HUMBLE YOURSELVES UNDER THE MIGHTY
> POWER OF GOD, AND IN HIS GOOD TIME
> HE WILL HONOR YOU.
> *1 Peter 5:5–6*

Five months earlier I had my act together. I had a great marriage, good kids, and a successful consulting business. Everything was going my way. Everything was on track. I owed it all to my skills, intelligence, business acumen, and a lot of hard work. I knew how to stand on my own two feet and didn't need any help from anyone. And I was still relatively attractive for a woman in her mid-forties . . . perfect size 8, long black hair, and I didn't even have to color. I even had God figured out. I went to church on Sunday, listened to all the messages, and thought I understood everything God had to show me. Today, I sat bald and broken on the bathroom floor. Stripped of every hair, stripped of every pride coat . . . humbled before God.

Jesus often reminded His followers that "those who exalt themselves will be humbled, and those who humble themselves will be exalted" (Matthew 23:12). In the ultimate act of servanthood, He humbled himself and became obedient even before death (Philippians 2:8). Think of it. The God who created the universe and set the stars in place chose to leave the comforts of heaven to come down to earth. He walked with us, lived with us, and ate with us. He suffered human pain and tasted human death. It is in His gentle and humble heart that we find rest for our weary souls and truly experience the love of God (Matthew 11:29). The humble act of obedience of one man gave us the keys to the heavenly mansion and direct access to the throne room of God. God honored the obedience of His Son by exalting Him to the highest position in heaven and earth.

Are you wearing any coats of pride? Perhaps you have been depending on your own strength instead of God's, or you've been busy doing your own thing instead of seeking Him. Perhaps you have been striving for success, seeking recognition, unwilling to ask for help, or unwilling to receive teaching or correction. The world might be impressed with your accomplishments, but God is more interested in your humility. When you are great in the world's eyes, you get the credit. But when He lifts you up, *He* gets the glory because the world sees all He has done for you. Perhaps today, this cancer has you on your knees. . . . bald and broken, with every coat of pride and every hair on your body stripped away. Today, it's just you and God. If you haven't already done so, invite Him into the center of your battle. When the heavenly Father looks into your heart and sees your genuine humility, He *will* honor you. ❦

TOTALLY UNCONDITIONAL

> LOVE IS PATIENT AND KIND. LOVE IS NOT
> JEALOUS OR BOASTFUL OR PROUD OR RUDE.
> LOVE DOES NOT DEMAND ITS OWN WAY.
> LOVE IS NOT IRRITABLE, AND IT KEEPS NO
> RECORD OF WHEN IT HAS BEEN WRONGED.
> IT IS NEVER GLAD ABOUT INJUSTICE BUT
> REJOICES WHENEVER THE TRUTH WINS OUT.
> LOVE NEVER GIVES UP, NEVER LOSES FAITH,
> IS ALWAYS HOPEFUL, AND ENDURES
> THROUGH EVERY CIRCUMSTANCE.
> *1 Corinthians 13:4–7*

One of my best role models for showing genuine love was my golden retriever. Regardless of how crummy I felt or how crabby I acted, Blazer loved me. When it felt like the whole world was crashing down, Blazer loved me. He loved when no one else could love me and when everyone else pulled away. He loved me when I couldn't love myself. When my hair started falling out, the entire time it took for my husband to shave my head, this sweet gentle dog lay on the floor and licked my feet. When I lay on the couch, sick from chemo, he nuzzled his head into my neck. It was just like he knew. He never expected anything in return. He simply loved. He was twelve years old when he went to romp in the heavenly fields. I felt like I had lost one of my best friends.

There is a love even greater than this that comes directly from the heart of God. It's the love we experience when the Holy Spirit dwells in us and the love we demonstrate to others as we become more and more like Christ (1 John 4:12, 17). God showed us this love when He sent His Son as a perfect sacrifice to take away our sins. God loves us, not because we deserve it, but because God *is* love. His very nature is love. His love is unconditional. He gives it to us freely without expecting anything in return, no matter how unworthy we might be. God used the simple love of a family pet to start teaching me about genuine God-quality, God-sized love.

Understanding how much God loves you makes it a lot easier to trust Him and to be in a personal relationship with Him. If you accept His unconditional love for you, you won't resent Him when a prayer goes unanswered or something doesn't work out as you had hoped. If you accept His unconditional love for you, you won't resent Him for this cancer. Instead, you will trust the One who loves you to always know what's best for you. You'll trust Him to have a much better plan for your life than you could conceive on your own. You'll trust He will use your cancer to draw you closer to His heart. His love for you is holy, just, and perfect. It endures through every circumstance. And it's totally unconditional. 🌾

New Tires

> He gives power to those who are tired and worn out; he offers strength to the weak. Even youths will become exhausted, and young men will give up. But those who wait on the Lord will find new strength. They will fly high on wings like eagles. They will run and not grow weary. They will walk and not faint.
>
> *Isaiah 40:29–31*

The afternoon of my first chemotherapy session I went shopping for new tires. My family had a fit. They expected me to go home to bed and rest, as people who have cancer are supposed to do. I felt fine, my car needed new tires, and I had some time that afternoon to shop, so why not? Three or four days from then, I wouldn't feel so great. But that afternoon I felt fine.

This pattern continued throughout my chemo. I tried my best to keep up my old pace. On many days I was able to walk my three miles. When I felt good I continued working. I probably pushed myself a little too hard sometimes. I've been known to be a bit stubborn. (Ask my family.) It was a blessing to be self-employed and have an office in the home. On more than one occasion I facilitated a client conference call with eight people on the line while sitting at my desk in my bald head and pj's. At the time, I probably thought it was my own determination that carried me through the fatigue and the chemo "creepy crawlies." Now I know the Holy Spirit had me covered like a blanket. Each new day, the Lord renewed my strength and gave power to my tired and worn-out body.

Fatigue may be one of the greatest challenges you face in living with your cancer treatment. Whether it's the chemo or the radiation, the trips to the clinic, or simply mental exhaustion, some days you will just be tired and worn out. How awesome to know you can depend on the Lord and He'll lift you high on wings like eagles! In His strength, you can crush an army or scale any wall (Psalm 18:29). In His strength, you can run and not grow weary. In His strength, you can walk and not grow faint. Sometimes you won't feel much like running. Other times, when your loved ones expect you to rest, you might feel up for a three-mile walk or trip to the mall. Go for it. Maybe you'll find a good deal on some tires. 🌾

A MILLION MILES AWAY

> MY GOD, MY GOD! WHY HAVE YOU
> FORSAKEN ME? WHY DO YOU REMAIN SO
> DISTANT? WHY DO YOU IGNORE MY CRIES
> FOR HELP? EVERY DAY I CALL TO YOU, MY
> GOD, BUT YOU DO NOT ANSWER. EVERY
> NIGHT YOU HEAR MY VOICE, BUT I FIND NO
> RELIEF. YET YOU ARE HOLY.
> *Psalm 22:1–3*

The night before my diagnosis was confirmed, I dropped on my knees in prayer in the middle of my office. In desperation, I cried out to God and surrendered the outcome of the tests to Him. His response was immediate. The Holy Spirit rained down on me, filling me from head to toe. There were no flames or tongues of fire, but it was a powerful, emotional, Pentecost-like experience. I felt tingly all over, and a supernatural peace covered me like a warm fuzzy blanket. Early in my cancer journey, this experience set the benchmark for my communication with God. I was distressed when I would come to Him in prayer and feel no emotion or hear nothing but silence. I started worrying He had forgotten me. At times, He seemed a million miles away.

God's silence during my cancer journey taught me that every encounter with Him would not be a Pentecost moment. Oddly, the silence actually strengthened my faith. If every prayer time ended in fireworks proving God's presence, what good would my faith be? Jesus said we are blessed if we believe without proof (John 20:29). The silent times actually helped me to press in and seek Him more. And I found the best way to get to know Him better is through His Word. Since Jesus *is* the Word (John 1:1), spending time in my Bible was like spending time with Jesus. As I meditated on His Word day and night and let it take over my thinking, eventually my emotions caught up. At times, it was Pentecost all over again.

There will be lonely days during the long weeks of chemotherapy and radiation when you cry out to God in prayer and hear nothing but an eerie silence. There will be days when you feel like your prayers are evaporating into the air. These are the days to press in. Spend time reading your Bible and meditating on the Word of God. Spend time in the presence of Jesus. His Word always produces fruit and it never comes back empty (Isaiah 55:11). Let the Word of Christ dwell in you richly (Colossians 3:16). You may hear fireworks. You may not. Yet He is holy. And He always hears. Even when He seems a million miles away. 𝕱

NO ESCAPE

I CAN NEVER ESCAPE FROM YOUR SPIRIT! I
CAN NEVER GET AWAY FROM YOUR
PRESENCE! IF I GO UP TO HEAVEN, YOU ARE
THERE; IF I GO DOWN TO THE PLACE OF THE
DEAD, YOU ARE THERE. IF I RIDE THE WINGS
OF THE MORNING, IF I DWELL BY THE
FARTHEST OCEANS, EVEN THERE YOUR HAND
WILL GUIDE ME, AND YOUR STRENGTH WILL
SUPPORT ME. I COULD ASK THE DARKNESS
TO HIDE ME AND THE LIGHT AROUND ME TO
BECOME NIGHT—BUT EVEN IN DARKNESS I
CANNOT HIDE FROM YOU. TO YOU THE
NIGHT SHINES AS BRIGHT AS DAY. DARKNESS
AND LIGHT ARE BOTH ALIKE TO YOU.
Psalm 139:7–12

The reality of my situation was slowly starting to sink in. I was no longer known as someone's wife, mom, sister, daughter, or friend. I was no longer the manager of this project or the chair of that committee or the one whose turn it was to have Thanksgiving dinner. I was the one with breast cancer. And I would wear this label for several months. As I emerged from the fog of disbelief swirling around me, I started noticing how people reacted to my new label. Some family members, like my sister, jumped in headfirst to help. Others pulled away or disappeared altogether. A former co-worker sobbed on the phone when I told her. (She was a nurse, so her reaction wasn't very comforting!) Friends who rarely call jumped back into my life, as though they had little time left to spend with me, and then disappeared again when it was all over.

I was most surprised by the people I've never met who wrote cards and letters and prayed for me. Family, friends . . . all reacting differently to my new label.

There was one whose reaction never changed. His reaction was the same before, during, and after my cancer. He saw me before I was born. He knit together the delicate, inner parts of my body. He recorded every day of my life in His book and laid out every moment before a single day had passed (Psalm 139:13–16). He gave me strength when I had none. He was my refuge when I was afraid. He was my friend when everyone scattered. He never left my side. Even if I tried, I could never escape Him. It would be foolish to try to hide from Him. He sees all and knows all. He is present everywhere. He is God.

Perhaps there are a few people in your life who are uncomfortable with your cancer and have been avoiding you. How awesome to know that when your friends and family scatter in several directions, God stays. He will never leave you or forsake you (Hebrews 13:5). Does it mean He no longer loves you because you have breast cancer? No, it's impossible for Christ to stop loving you. He died on the cross for you, and all the powers of heaven and hell can't keep His love away (Romans 8:35–39). No matter what you do or where you go, you can't get away from God or His love. There's simply no escape. 🌸

HAZARDOUS TO YOUR HEALTH

THEY VISIT ME AS IF THEY ARE MY FRIENDS,
BUT ALL THE WHILE THEY GATHER GOSSIP,
AND WHEN THEY LEAVE, THEY SPREAD IT
EVERYWHERE. ALL WHO HATE ME WHISPER
ABOUT ME, IMAGINING THE WORST FOR ME.
"WHATEVER HE HAS, IT IS FATAL," THEY SAY.
"HE WILL NEVER GET OUT OF THAT BED!"
Psalm 41:6–8

Oh dear, you're the one with breast cancer. These were the first words out of the mouth of a woman I met at a family function. I looked around and saw no one behind me, so I assumed she was talking to me. It was shortly after my surgery but before my chemo started, so I still had my hair and my self-esteem intact. She proceeded to tell me about her friends and relatives who had died of breast cancer and how sorry she was for me. The look on her face was one of someone paying last respects at a friend's deathbed. Every time I ran into her, she approached me with that same sad, foreboding look. *Hang in there, dear.* Hang where? I don't know about you, lady, but I'm not going anywhere. I started running for cover whenever I saw her coming.

The people I spent time with had a profound influence on my cancer recovery. They could either build up my faith or tear it down. When in the presence of skeptics who doubted my healing and assumed the worst, I was tempted to doubt the Word of God and His healing promises. When faithful believers who spoke God's truth surrounded me, I was lifted and filled with hope. I quickly learned to avoid those whose thoughts and beliefs contradicted God and dishonored His Word.

As you prepare to meet your cancer today, take a look at the company you keep. Do you surround yourself with those who draw you closer to God or those who drag you down into defeat? There are many who would claim to be religious but reject the power of Christ (2 Timothy 3:5). Follow God's truth and turn your back on the skeptics who say the Lord will never rescue you. Instead, spend your time with true believers who call out to God with a pure heart (2 Timothy 2:22). Let their faith encourage and build you up. Hanging out with anyone else may be hazardous to your health. ❦

THROW AWAY THE KEY

> WE DEMOLISH ARGUMENTS AND EVERY
> PRETENSION THAT SETS ITSELF UP AGAINST
> THE KNOWLEDGE OF GOD, AND WE TAKE
> CAPTIVE EVERY THOUGHT TO MAKE IT
> OBEDIENT TO CHRIST.
> *2 Corinthians 10:5* NIV

It still happens, even though it's been five years since I was treated for stage 2 breast cancer. A little voice tries to whisper in my ear while I'm in bed at night. *You don't really believe you're healed, do you?* Sometimes it sneaks up on me when I'm praying for someone who is going through cancer treatment, or when my back starts aching from sitting at my computer for too long. Sometimes I hear it when my husband and I are daydreaming about our future. When we retire, we'll ride our Gold Wing into the sunset, or we'll buy a cabin on the lake for our grandkids, or we'll rent a villa in Tuscany for the summer. *You don't really think you'll still be around, do you?*

Until I understood the source of these lies they threw me into a panic. Now I understand. As a Christian, my battle is not against flesh and blood but against the evil rulers and authorities of the unseen world (Ephesians 6:10–12). But I have nothing to fear. God gave me His Holy Spirit and His protective armor so I can stand firm and resist the enemy (Ephesians 6:13–18). And He gave me a supernatural weapon against all the lies of darkness. He gave me His Word. Christ used it as His weapon when He was tempted in the desert (Matthew 4:1–10). And the Word of God tells me I can take every whispering lie and command it captive under the authority and obedience of Jesus Christ. Poof. Gone. Just like that.

There is another battlefield as you fight your cancer today. It's the battlefield of your mind. Anything that comes into it that is contrary to the Word of God did not come from Him. It comes from the greatest deceiver of all time. The devil, our great enemy, prowls around like a roaring lion looking for some victim to devour (1 Peter 5:8–9). Guess what? Your God is bigger and stronger and His Son already won. He defeated the father of darkness on the cross at Calvary. You have the power to stop the lie in its tracks. Refuse to accept it. Take every lie captive under the authority of Jesus Christ. Lock it up and throw away the key.

GOD BREATHED

> ALL SCRIPTURE IS INSPIRED BY GOD AND IS
> USEFUL TO TEACH US WHAT IS TRUE AND TO
> MAKE US REALIZE WHAT IS WRONG IN OUR
> LIVES. IT STRAIGHTENS US OUT AND TEACHES
> US TO DO WHAT IS RIGHT. IT IS GOD'S WAY
> OF PREPARING US IN EVERY WAY, FULLY
> EQUIPPED FOR EVERY GOOD THING
> GOD WANTS US TO DO.
> *2 Timothy 3:16–17*

I had every healing promise underlined in my study Bible.

* "O Lord my God, I cried out to you for help, and you restored my health" (Psalm 30:2).
* "For I am the Lord who heals you" (Exodus 15:26).
* "He forgives all my sins and heals all my diseases" (Psalm 103:3).
* "'I will give you back your health and heal your wounds,' says the Lord" (Jeremiah 30:17).

But Lord, do you still heal today? Is the Bible still true? I wanted desperately to believe it. In spite of several warnings not to tamper with God's Word (Revelations 22:18–19; Deuteronomy 4:1–4), we are tempted to pull out the things we want to believe and ignore the things we don't. It seems like some scholars have even tried to elevate their human interpretation to the same level of authority as the Bible itself. If this part is outdated, perhaps that part is outdated too? God's Word is the final authority . . . sometimes? When? Who decides? Where does it stop? Suddenly, instead of black and white, it becomes gray and confusing. And confusion creates doubt.

As you meditate on His words of healing today, know that the Bible is not a human book. It is beautifully written, but it is not literature or a collection of stories and fables. It is the inspired Word of God. God revealed himself and His plan to certain believers through the Holy Spirit who wrote down His message from their own historical and cultural contexts. They wrote what *He* wanted them to write. So when I read His Word, I know it's trustworthy. His Word is my standard for testing everything else that claims to be true. It is my safeguard against false teaching and my guiding light for how to live. It reveals the true character of God and the full life I can have in His presence.

I know what you might be thinking. *But what about the part where it says . . .* Just because we can't or won't follow the Bible's teaching perfectly, or we are perplexed by some of it, doesn't mean it isn't truth. It simply means we can't or won't follow God's Word to a tee. And this is no surprise to God. We all sin and fall short of His glorious standard (Romans 3:23). That's exactly the reason He gave us a Savior. So you can hang your hat on every word and every healing promise you read in His book. Every word is truth. Every word is God breathed. 🌿

Let the Party Begin!

His son said to him, "Father, I have sinned against both heaven and you, and I am no longer worthy of being called your son." But his father said to the servants, "Quick! Bring the finest robe in the house and put it on him. Get a ring for his finger, and sandals for his feet. And kill the calf we have been fattening in the pen. We must celebrate with a feast, for this son of mine was dead and has now returned to life. He was lost, but now he is found." So the party began.

Luke 15:21–24

The young woman looked at me with deep sorrow in her eyes when I offered to pray for her. She had just had a mastectomy, and the pathology report confirmed thirteen positive nodes out of thirteen. Her doctor had ordered a CT scan and a bone scan and had prepared her for the strong possibility that the cancer had spread to her other organs. *But you don't understand. I haven't been to church since I was a little girl in Sunday school. I haven't paid any attention to God. Why should He help me now, just because I'm in trouble? I feel guilty even asking.*

I'm sure the lost son in Jesus' parable felt the same way about returning to his earthly father. After squandering all his inheritance on wild living, he was so poor and hungry he was forced to eat with the pigs. Pigs were unclean according to Moses' law, so he had truly sunk to the depths of humiliation. When he came to his senses, he returned to his father who ran to him with open arms and threw a party to celebrate his safe return.

This young rebellious son had wanted to be free and live as he pleased. He had to hit rock bottom to seek his father's help. Our relationship with our heavenly Father is much the same. He will give us plenty of opportunities to come to Him, but He won't force us to respond. We might have to experience a great sorrow like breast cancer to look to Him for help. But our Father is full of love and patience. When we finally come home, He welcomes us with open arms, no matter how long we've been gone.

Like the lost son in the parable, this same young woman humbled herself before her Father that night in the prayer chapel. She asked Him to forgive all her years of indifference and rebellion. She invited Christ into her life and into the center of her cancer. You could almost hear the angels clapping and cheering in heaven when she came back home. And do you know what? She called a couple days later. There was no cancer in her bones or liver, or anywhere else in her body. It was limited to her breast and her lymph nodes. Her doctor was amazed.

Have you been away from home too long? Are you feeling unworthy? Your Father in heaven created you just a little lower than himself and the angels (Psalm 8:3–6). You are highly valuable to Him, even when you disappoint Him, even if you've been out of touch for a while. His great love will reach out and welcome you home, regardless of where you've been or how long you've been gone. Listen closely. Can you hear the angels clapping and cheering? A daughter was lost, but now she is found! Let the party begin! ❧

THE GOD OF YOUR PARKING PLACE

> THE STEPS OF THE GODLY ARE DIRECTED BY
> THE LORD. HE DELIGHTS IN EVERY DETAIL
> OF THEIR LIVES. THOUGH THEY STUMBLE,
> THEY WILL NOT FALL, FOR THE LORD HOLDS
> THEM BY THE HAND.
> *Psalm 37:23–24*

I grew up believing that God didn't want to be bothered with the little things. I thought mundane everyday concerns, like where I put my car keys or my glasses, the meeting I had to lead at work tomorrow, my son's hockey game, or the meal I had to prepare for Christmas Eve were too insignificant for His busy schedule. Our churches often perpetuate this belief. Posted prayer lists will often be limited to the sick and hospitalized, people in the military, or those suffering the loss of a loved one. When my cancer was diagnosed, I felt qualified to go before my Father in heaven with my request. It was a big one.

There is an interesting story in the Old Testament about God's care and provision for those who trust Him (2 Kings 6:1–6). The prophet Elisha and his students went down to the Jordan River to cut some trees to build a new meeting place. While chopping, one of the young prophets lost his ax head in the river. He cried out in despair to Elisha, because he had borrowed the ax. Elisha simply threw a stick in the water and the ax head floated to the top of the surface. Relieved, the young man reached out and grabbed it.

Did God really care about the lost ax head enough to raise it from the bottom of the river to the surface? Yes! When God said pray about everything, He meant *everything* (Philippians 4:6). His Word doesn't say pray about *some* things or pray about the really *important* things. So don't limit God to prayers for healing or good test results. You can pray about every worry or concern on your heart, no matter how insignificant you think it might be. Maybe you need someone to watch your kids while you go to the doctor. Maybe you long for a nice family dinner together with no interruptions. Maybe it's something silly, like getting your eyebrows painted on straight before you leave for work in the morning. Pray! Your Father delights in *every* detail of your life. He wants to be the God of your parking place! ❧

DONE DEAL

CAN WE BOAST, THEN, THAT WE HAVE DONE
ANYTHING TO BE ACCEPTED BY GOD?
NO, BECAUSE OUR ACQUITTAL IS NOT BASED
ON OUR GOOD DEEDS. IT IS BASED ON OUR
FAITH. SO WE ARE MADE RIGHT WITH GOD
THROUGH FAITH AND NOT BY
OBEYING THE LAW.
Romans 3:27–28

It was just another Sunday afternoon at the Vikings game. As season ticket holders for several years, our family settled into the same seats, all decked out in our game jerseys and ready to cheer on the boys in purple. But today was different. Today I was bald. I wore an elastic band around my head with a fringe of hair attached, and topped off the entire comical affair with my Vikings cap. I prayed I wouldn't have to remove my cap for the national anthem. I prayed the rowdy crowd wouldn't knock it off my head. *Lord, am I the only one in this stadium of 64,000 screaming fans who is trying desperately to hide the effects of chemotherapy? Lord, I've been a good person. What did I do to deserve this?*

At some point in my faith journey, I realized no one was sitting in heaven keeping track of my good deeds and handing out brownie points. I couldn't earn my way into God's favor. It's not about what I *do*. How will I ever know when I've done enough or been good enough? It's all about what's been *done* for me. Jesus died. He died because I could never do enough. Because I'm human, I can't possibly follow all the rules. No one can (Romans 3:23). The more I learned about God's character and His law, the clearer it became I couldn't obey it (Romans 3:20). If you don't believe me, take a walk through the Old Testament. I can only be made right with God by trusting Christ to take away my sins (Romans 3:22–23). In this one ultimate act of love, God wiped my record clean (Romans 3:24). It doesn't matter how good I am. If it did, the only one in heaven would be Jesus. The rest of us would be keeping each other company in the fiery lake.

No, I didn't deserve breast cancer, and neither do you. But think of this: It is only by the grace of God that we receive every blessing in our lives. And it's only by His mercy that we aren't penalized for every sin. No good deed would have prevented your breast cancer. No amount of personal achievement or personal goodness will ever bridge the gap between our human imperfection and God's perfection. Only by trusting what God has done for you at the Cross will you be made whole and perfect in His sight (Ephesians 2:8–10). Have you accepted His love offering? You don't have to *do* anything to earn it; it's a done deal. ❧

He Conquered Every One

HERE ON EARTH YOU WILL HAVE MANY
TRIALS AND SORROWS. BUT TAKE HEART,
BECAUSE I HAVE OVERCOME THE WORLD.
John 16:33

It was a beautiful sunny afternoon in early January, about seven months after I finished my final chemo and radiation. I was feeling great, working out every day, and had even incorporated some free weights into my routine. The worst was behind me and I was daydreaming about the new year ahead and all the things I might do now that my life was back to normal. I didn't notice the black icy patch in the shadow of the car parked next to me. When I stepped out of my car to go into the store, I stepped on the ice and slipped. I don't remember much after that, except my kneecap was twisted around to the back of my leg, the pain was excruciating, there were people all around me, including some police officers and EMTs who were trying to load me into an ambulance. Two years later—including several months of physical therapy and one surgery—I regained total function in my right knee.

People said I should be angry. After all I had been through the past year I didn't deserve this. Besides, my cancer had brought me into a closer personal relationship with Jesus Christ. Shouldn't I have a special dispensation from pain and suffering, at least for a time? Being a Christian with a personal relationship with the Savior doesn't guarantee an easy, problem-free life. It *does* guarantee direct access to His supernatural peace and comfort in the midst of our trials. We will be pressed on every side by troubles, but He promises we will never be crushed and broken. We may be confused and under attack, but He promises never to abandon us. We may even fall in an icy parking lot, but with His strength, we get up again and keep on going. When our perishable earthly bodies suffer, we share in the death of Jesus. But we also share in His victory. Every trial is an opportunity for Christ to show us His power and shine His light through us (2 Corinthians 4:8–10).

It would have been nice to avoid the knee fiasco. I pray you don't suffer a similar ordeal when your treatment ends and the road ahead looks wide open for the first time in months. When you became a Christian, you secured your eternity in Jesus Christ. But that didn't make you exempt from the world's problems. Take heart! He left you with a precious gift. You have the deep and everlasting peace of Christ within you. It's a peace not of this world (John 14:27). You have His confident assurance in *every* trial, in *every* sorrow the world throws at you. He conquered every one. ❧

BLESSINGS FROM HEAVEN

YOU WILL EXPERIENCE ALL THESE BLESSINGS
IF YOU OBEY THE LORD YOUR GOD: YOU
WILL BE BLESSED IN YOUR TOWNS AND IN
THE COUNTRY. YOU WILL BE BLESSED WITH
MANY CHILDREN AND PRODUCTIVE FIELDS.
YOU WILL BE BLESSED WITH FERTILE HERDS
AND FLOCKS. YOU WILL BE BLESSED WITH
BASKETS OVERFLOWING WITH FRUIT, AND
WITH KNEADING BOWLS FILLED WITH BREAD.
YOU WILL BE BLESSED WHEREVER YOU GO,
BOTH IN COMING AND IN GOING.

Deuteronomy 28:2–6

The diagnosis and surgery behind me, I started preparing for the difficult weeks and months ahead. I adjusted my work schedule, cleared some family commitments, and attended chemo class. Then the real challenge began. I started shopping for hats and wigs. I wore my long black hair parted on the side with no bangs, and soon discovered it would be difficult to replace with a natural-looking wig. So I bought a cute short one and had my hair cut and styled to match the wig. Later, when I lost my hair and transitioned into the wig, no one was the wiser. The wig worked fine for work and more formal outings, but not for casual days or walking at the club. So I got creative. I found a fringe of hair about six inches long attached to a Velcro strip and sewed a matching Velcro strip into all my caps. It worked great, except if I removed my cap, the hair went with it! Even so, I had fashioned quite a hair replacement system.

On Thanksgiving it was time to make my public debut. I selected one of my caps, carefully Velcroed my "hair" in place, and headed home. As we sat around the Thanksgiving table, I was not alone. With a little undercover planning by my sister, everyone surprised me by wearing a cap. It was an expression of God's love through my family, just when I needed it most. In the middle of my cancer, He prepared a feast for me and welcomed me as the honored guest. My cup overflowed with blessing (Psalm 23:5)!

God enjoys surprising you with gifts, just as an earthly parent does. When you walk with Him and obey Him, He *wants* to bless you. Every good and perfect thing comes from Him (James 1:17). Yes, even the little insignificant things. Like a Thanksgiving dinner with fourteen loved ones, each wearing a different hat in your honor. Maybe your whole family will shave their heads right along with you. Blessings come from obeying God and seeking Him every day. Thank Him for His unfailing love and faithfulness expressed through His Son. And prepare to receive one gracious blessing after another (John 1:16–17). Blessings from heaven. 🦢

YOUR POWER SOURCE

> BUT THIS PRECIOUS TREASURE—THIS LIGHT
> AND POWER THAT NOW SHINE WITHIN US—
> IS HELD IN PERISHABLE CONTAINERS, THAT
> IS, IN OUR WEAK BODIES. SO EVERYONE CAN
> SEE THAT OUR GLORIOUS POWER IS FROM
> GOD AND IS NOT OUR OWN.
>
> *2 Corinthians 4:7*

*P*eople were amazed at my positive attitude. My oncologist's nurse was the first to notice it. *You'll do fine. You have a great attitude.* My friends told other friends. *She's doing great. She's so optimistic!* Family members discussed it among themselves. *She never complains. She has such a positive attitude.* By all the world's standards, there was nothing to be positive about. But my outward persona and the words and actions witnessed by my family and friends were not of this world.

There are some who would still give me all the credit for the strong and optimistic woman they observed during my breast cancer experience, but nothing they observed came from my own strength and abilities. I was just a weak and fallible human being— a perishable container—holding on for dear life to the precious treasure deep inside my heart. The Holy Spirit sustained me through every minute of my cancer. His light and power shined within and through me. He gave me a new song to sing! And when the people around me saw what He had done, they were astounded (Psalm 40:3).

When God has His rightful place in the center of your cancer, you can't help but give public praise to the silent work He is doing in the depths of your heart (Psalm 22:22). People will be amazed when you don't complain. They will be astounded when you shine brightly through the darkness of your cancer. A transformed life and an attitude that defies all the world's expectations are effective testimony to the power of the Holy Spirit dwelling richly inside you (Philippians 2:14–15). In the midst of all the chemo sessions, the needles, the nausea, and the baldness, let the light of Christ shine through. Let the world see your power source. ✢

HOLY GROUND

> THEN JESUS UTTERED ANOTHER LOUD CRY
> AND BREATHED HIS LAST. AND THE CURTAIN
> IN THE TEMPLE WAS TORN IN TWO, FROM
> TOP TO BOTTOM.
> *Mark 15:37–38*

*M*y cancer made me hunger more for the Word of God. When our church offered a daily reading program that promised to guide me through the entire Bible in a year, I jumped at the opportunity to participate. (Besides, I thought it might provide the incentive I needed to get through the Old Testament.) In studying the Law of Moses, I learned about a heavy curtain that hung in the Temple at the entrance between the Holy Place and the Most Holy Place. The curtain prevented anyone from entering or even catching a glimpse into the place God reserved for himself. Once a year, the high priest was allowed to enter the Most Holy Place and stand in God's presence as he made a blood sacrifice to gain forgiveness for the sins of the nation. The curtain represented the separation between the holy and righteous God and the sinful people (Leviticus 16; Hebrews 9:1–14).

For a long time I didn't fully grasp the significance of the curtain tearing when Jesus drew His last breath. I knew it was the blood of Christ, not the blood of goats and calves, that secured my salvation forever (Hebrews 9:12). One night during Lent, while praying for a woman with breast cancer, the rest of the story became clear. The only reason I can come before God in prayer is because of Christ's ultimate sacrifice. At the moment of His death, the curtain was torn in two, symbolizing that the barrier between

God and humanity was removed. His death opened the sacred curtain so all could freely enter His presence (Hebrews 10:20). He was whipped and beaten. He hauled the cross up the hill to Calvary. He spilled innocent blood, just to make me pure and holy and worthy of coming into the presence of His Father (Hebrews 10:22).

Just think of it! Christ died for you on a cross to give you eternal life. But you don't have to wait until you leave this earth to bask in His eternal glory. You have unlimited free admission into heaven's Most Holy Place (Hebrews 10:19). Right here, right now. You don't have to be a priest or a prophet. You don't have to be rich or famous. You can go fearlessly into His presence and be assured of a glad welcome (Ephesians 3:12). Once you fully understand the price Jesus paid so you could spend time with His heavenly Father, you will never approach prayer in the same way again. Every time you bow your head, every time you cry out for healing, every time you ask Him to lighten the load of your cancer, you are standing on holy ground—holy ground bought and paid for by the blood of Christ. *

A CHILD'S FAITH

> ONE DAY SOME PARENTS BROUGHT THEIR
> CHILDREN TO JESUS SO HE COULD TOUCH
> THEM AND BLESS THEM, BUT THE DISCIPLES
> TOLD THEM NOT TO BOTHER HIM. BUT
> WHEN JESUS SAW WHAT WAS HAPPENING, HE
> WAS VERY DISPLEASED WITH HIS DISCIPLES.
> HE SAID TO THEM, "LET THE CHILDREN
> COME TO ME. DON'T STOP THEM! FOR THE
> KINGDOM OF GOD BELONGS TO SUCH AS
> THESE. I ASSURE YOU, ANYONE WHO
> DOESN'T HAVE THEIR KIND OF FAITH WILL
> NEVER GET INTO THE KINGDOM OF GOD."
> *Mark 10:13–15*

Perhaps, like me, you've heard stories about missionaries who go deep into remote tribal areas of the world to spread the Good News. People with every disease and infirmity come from miles around to hear about this man called Jesus. When they accept Him as Lord and Savior and receive prayer for healing, they are healed *en masse*. The mute speak, the blind see, the deaf hear, and the lame walk, just as in the Gospels and the early church (Matthew 9:20–22, 27–31; 14:34–36; 15:29–31; Acts 3:6–8; 5:16). And the crowds are amazed by what they have seen.

In my quest for healing, I often wondered what is so different about these believers. I wondered if their new faith is like the children's faith that Jesus commended. Children need little more than kindness and a gentle touch to trust the adults who care for them. Their faith is pure and simple and defies grown-up logic. Most children haven't yet experienced the hypocrisy, inconsistencies, and even some of the religious traditions that cast doubt on the beliefs of many adults. When children are taught about God's will to heal those who love Him because He says so in His Word, they won't point out ten examples of when He didn't. When children are taught about the healing miracles in the Bible, they simply believe it. We adults often look upon modern-day miracles with skepticism, even though the Word clearly says God never changes (Malachi 3:6; Hebrews 13:8). Jesus said we would do even greater miracles than these, and that we would be able to place our hands on the sick and heal them (Matthew 21:21; Mark 16:17–18). Yet we sit back with our arms crossed . . . doubting and wondering.

As you meet your cancer today, imagine your faith is like a child's. You don't need to understand all the mysteries of God's kingdom and solve all the apparent inconsistencies around you to believe His Word. You simply need to know He loves you, and that's enough. Like a child, you come before Him with a humble and sincere heart, weak and dependent on Him for your every need (Matthew 18:4–5). You believe it's His will to heal you. You believe in miracles. You come to Him with a child's faith. Be prepared to be amazed. The Kingdom of God belongs to you. 🦋

THANK YOU, LORD!

IT IS GOOD TO GIVE THANKS TO THE LORD,
TO SING PRAISES TO THE MOST HIGH. IT IS
GOOD TO PROCLAIM YOUR UNFAILING LOVE
IN THE MORNING, YOUR FAITHFULNESS IN
THE EVENING, ACCOMPANIED BY THE HARP
AND LUTE AND THE HARMONY OF THE LYRE.
YOU THRILL ME, LORD, WITH ALL YOU HAVE
DONE FOR ME! I SING FOR JOY BECAUSE OF
WHAT YOU HAVE DONE.

Psalm 92:1–4

What did I have to be thankful about? Not the call from my doctor with the results of my biopsy. *You have invasive breast cancer.* Or the surgeon's report in the recovery room. *You had two positive nodes.* Or my first visit to the oncologist. *Since your cancer is stage 2, you need eight cycles of chemotherapy, three weeks apart. And yes, you'll lose all your hair.* It wasn't the drugs, IV drips, needles, and blood tests . . . week after week, over and over again. Yet, in the middle of my suffering, there were good reasons to be thankful. It was a miracle the cancer was discovered in the first place. My doctor persisted, even when the mammogram came back negative. The tumor was small, the margins were negative, and the surgeon did an outstanding job preserving my breast. As for my chemo, I loved my oncologist, the side effects were manageable, and I was able to stay active. And there were little blessings . . . I got a break from shaving my legs and my wig was kind of cute. Thank you, Lord!

Jesus healed ten lepers, all who had good reasons to be

thankful. People with leprosy were completely cut off from society and lived miserable, lonely lives. Jesus sent all ten lepers to the priest to be declared clean as required by the Law of Moses. On the way to the priest, their leprosy disappeared. Since they responded in faith, Jesus healed them. But only one leper returned to thank Jesus. Since he responded with a grateful heart, Jesus revealed to this man that his faith had healed him (Luke 17:15–19). We too can grow closer to the mind of Christ through a thankful spirit. When we thank Him for all He has done, even in the midst of our cancer, we experience God's supernatural peace (Philippians 4:6–7). Eventually our attitudes start to change. We become more gracious, more humble, more loving . . . more like Christ.

So let your life overflow with thanksgiving (Colossians 2:7)! Thank Him for the technology that made your diagnosis possible. Thank Him for the skilled doctors and nurses who care for you. Thank Him for medical science and all the new drugs and treatment options that weren't available to women twenty years ago. Thank Him for friends and family who love you and pray for you. Think about how much He has helped you and sing for joy in the shadow of His protecting wings (Psalm 63:7). Sing praises in the morning. Sing praises in the evening. Thank you, Lord, for all you have done! 🌿

Dare to Believe

> As it is written: "I have made you a father of many nations." He is our father in the sight of God, in whom he believed—the God who gives life to the dead and calls things that are not as though they were.
>
> *Romans 4:17* NIV

When Abraham was already an old man, God promised to give him a son and make his descendents as numerous as the stars (Genesis 15:4–5). Several years later, when he was a man of ninety-nine years and his wife Sarah was old and still barren, God promised again to make him the father of many nations (Genesis 17: 4). He even changed his name from Abram to Abraham, which meant "father of many" (Genesis 17:5). Abraham never doubted that God would keep His promise. He was fully persuaded, absolutely convinced that God would do what He said He would do (Romans 4:20–21). God honored his faithfulness. Sarah finally bore him a son and the promise was fulfilled through Jesus Christ who came from Abraham's line.

Abraham believed in a God who simply spoke and the world appeared at His command (Psalm 33:8–9). He spoke and the entire universe was formed out of nothing (Hebrews 11:3). When He called Abraham the father of many nations years before it came to pass, He called into reality things that are not as though they were. And Abraham believed. He didn't deny his circumstances. He didn't say, "I'm not old." He simply believed God would do what only God could do. As I meditated on healing Scriptures, I noticed His Word doesn't say, "You *will be* healed by His wounds!" It doesn't say, "You *might be* healed by His wounds." It says, "You *have been* healed by His wounds" (1 Peter 2:24, emphasis added)! Past tense. Already done. If Abraham dared to believe God's promise of a son in spite of his obvious circumstances, could I dare to believe God's promise of healing before it became a reality?

Think of it! Abraham was old and childless, but God called him the father of many nations. He blessed the whole world when His promise became manifest. You have breast cancer, but God called you healed. No, the reality may not yet be proven in your body. You may still be bald and tired of chemo and doctors. But your God made the heavens and the earth! He gives life to the dead and calls things into existence out of nothing. By believing His promise of healing, you're not denying your breast cancer. You're simply denying its right to exist in you. Christ already rescued you from it on the cross (Galatians 3:13; Colossians 1:13–14). He carried it on His back on the road to Calvary (Isaiah 53:4–5). His wounds have healed you. Already done. Dare to believe it! ❧

WOMAN, WHY ARE YOU CRYING?

MARY STOOD OUTSIDE THE TOMB CRYING.
AS SHE WEPT, SHE BENT OVER TO LOOK
INTO THE TOMB AND SAW TWO ANGELS IN
WHITE, SEATED WHERE JESUS' BODY HAD
BEEN, ONE AT THE HEAD AND THE OTHER AT
THE FOOT. THEY ASKED HER, "WOMAN,
WHY ARE YOU CRYING?" "THEY HAVE
TAKEN MY LORD AWAY," SHE SAID, "AND I
DON'T KNOW WHERE THEY HAVE PUT HIM."
AT THIS, SHE TURNED AROUND AND SAW
JESUS STANDING THERE, BUT SHE DID NOT
REALIZE THAT IT WAS JESUS. "WOMAN," HE
SAID, "WHY ARE YOU CRYING? WHO IS IT
YOU ARE LOOKING FOR?" THINKING HE WAS
THE GARDENER, SHE SAID, "SIR, IF YOU HAVE
CARRIED HIM AWAY, TELL ME WHERE YOU
HAVE PUT HIM, AND I WILL GET HIM." JESUS
SAID TO HER, "MARY." SHE TURNED
TOWARD HIM AND CRIED OUT IN ARAMAIC,
"RABBONI!" (WHICH MEANS TEACHER).
John 20:11–16 NIV

He was there all the time. I was just too busy to hear Him calling my name. I didn't recognize His voice among all the others in the hustle and bustle of everyday life. Then my world exploded. It was quite likely the lump was cancerous. I frantically exhausted every worldly resource, as though my knowledge would provide the answer. No answer came. Only silence. All the voices were silent, except the small voice in my head. *Woman, why are you crying?* I had to come face-to-face with the fear of death before I recognized the voice of God. For the first time in my faith journey, the Lord was real. He was personal. He was alive.

Mary Magdalene didn't recognize the Lord at first. Her grief over His violent death on the cross blinded her to His resurrection. At first she thought He was the gardener, but when He spoke her name she knew immediately it was Jesus. She knew at that moment that He was indeed the risen Christ, the ruler of God's Kingdom, and He would accomplish all He had promised. She was filled with joy and responded in obedience by running to tell the disciples the Good News (John 20:18).

Have you discovered the empty grave? By the power of the resurrection, Jesus defeated death so you can live with Him forever in eternity. His resurrection power promised a full and abundant life on this earth from the moment you first believed (John 10:10). This same resurrection power dwells *within* you (Romans 8:11). Think of it! The Spirit of the living God is as close as your beating heart. You may be blinded by the grief of your cancer. Like the psalmist, you may be weak from sobbing and your pillow may be wet with weeping (Psalm 6:6–7). Listen. Can you hear your Savior calling your name? He's standing right next to you. Hallelujah! He's alive! Woman, why are you crying? ❧

I LOOK UP TO THE MOUNTAINS—DOES MY
HELP COME FROM THERE? MY HELP COMES
FROM THE LORD, WHO MADE THE HEAVENS
AND THE EARTH! HE WILL NOT LET YOU
STUMBLE AND FALL; THE ONE WHO WATCHES
OVER YOU WILL NOT SLEEP. INDEED, HE
WHO WATCHES OVER ISRAEL NEVER TIRES
AND NEVER SLEEPS. THE LORD HIMSELF
WATCHES OVER YOU! THE LORD STANDS
BESIDE YOU AS YOUR PROTECTIVE SHADE.
THE SUN WILL NOT HURT YOU BY DAY, NOR
THE MOON AT NIGHT. THE LORD KEEPS YOU
FROM ALL EVIL AND PRESERVES YOUR LIFE.
THE LORD KEEPS WATCH OVER YOU AS YOU
COME AND GO, BOTH NOW AND FOREVER.
Psalm 121

*G*oing through the treatment, I almost felt protected. The surgery removed the cancer. The chemo destroyed any microscopic cells that may have spread to the rest of my body, and the radiation made sure there was no cancer left in my breast. It felt good to be *doing* something to fight back. The weekly trips to the oncologist, the daily trips to the radiation clinic had become part of my routine. I enjoyed the time spent with my sister who took me to every treatment. I was even growing fond of the doctor, his nurse, and the rest of the staff who took care of me. Then it ended as abruptly as it started. My doctor handed me a prescription for an estrogen blocker, told me to come back in three months, and bid me farewell. *Now what?* For the first time in eight months, I felt exposed and vulnerable. I started taking vitamins and made some changes in my diet and exercise habits. *Am I doing enough to keep the cancer away? What else can I do to protect myself?*

Psalm 121 tells me where my true protection comes from. It's not from anything He created. My help comes from the Creator himself, the one who made the heavens and earth. The one who never tires and never sleeps. Today, as I live on the other side of my cancer, the Lord himself is my protective shade. Like supernatural sunscreen, He shields me from the searing sun and the scorching desert winds (Isaiah 49:10). Day and night He keeps watch against anything that would steal my health. There is nothing in all creation—no drug, no doctor, no checkup or test—that promises round-the-clock protection like the Lord can promise.

When your treatment is over and your doctors release you from their close supervision, you can take comfort in knowing your God is always on duty. He is the all-powerful God who created the universe, yet nothing diverts His attention away from you. You are always safe under the shelter of His wings. His protective shield covers you day and night (Psalm 91:4). You can look to the mountains. You can look to the doctors, the drugs, and the medical breakthroughs He creates. But your help comes from the Lord, the one who made the heavens and the earth and has authority over all things. He never sleeps. ❦

HOLY HOT FLASH

> ON THE DAY OF PENTECOST, SEVEN WEEKS
> AFTER JESUS' RESURRECTION, THE BELIEVERS
> WERE MEETING TOGETHER IN ONE PLACE.
> SUDDENLY, THERE WAS A SOUND FROM
> HEAVEN LIKE THE ROARING OF A MIGHTY
> WINDSTORM IN THE SKIES ABOVE THEM, AND
> IT FILLED THE HOUSE WHERE THEY WERE
> MEETING. THEN, WHAT LOOKED LIKE FLAMES
> OR TONGUES OF FIRE APPEARED AND
> SETTLED ON EACH OF THEM. AND EVERYONE
> PRESENT WAS FILLED WITH THE HOLY SPIRIT
> AND BEGAN SPEAKING IN OTHER LANGUAGES,
> AS THE HOLY SPIRIT GAVE THEM
> THIS ABILITY.
> *Acts 2:1–4*

With chemo came instant menopause. With menopause came instant hot flashes. If you haven't experienced them yet, you probably will. The worst is at night. I crawl into bed and snuggle under the covers. The next thing I know, the covers are on the floor and I'm drenched in sweat. Covers on, covers off. The cycle repeats until morning. I've been known to stand outside in the sub-zero Minnesota winter in pajamas. I've even been caught with my head in the freezer. I can't dry my hair without cold packs around my neck. If anyone knows how to put makeup on a wet face, let me know. Some joke that my hot flashes are really a filling of the Holy Spirit. If flames of fire are the norm, I'm one Spirit-filled, powered-up woman!

After Jesus ascended into heaven, God filled the first Christians with the Holy Spirit by sending a mighty windstorm and tongues of fire onto each of them. This fulfilled Jesus' promise that He would give every believer a Counselor who will never leave us (John 14:16). To have the Holy Spirit is to have Jesus himself living inside us (John 14:17). He's a powerful ally who teaches us as He taught the disciples (John 14:26). He guides us in all our decisions and reveals to us exactly what the Father wants Him to reveal (John 16:13). In faith, the Holy Spirit draws us close to the very heart and mind of God.

Have you checked in with your personal Savior lately? When we stay connected in prayer, Jesus talks to us through the Holy Spirit (John 16:13–15). He may speak through a prompting to call someone or do something. Perhaps it's a warning or a sudden answer to a problem you've been struggling to solve. Or perhaps He's been silent or you're just too heartbroken to pray. Don't despair. Even then, the Holy Spirit helps you in your distress. He pleads for you to the Father when you can't find the words (Romans 8:26–27). If you're having a dry spell, stop right now and pray for a fresh filling of His Spirit. But watch out. You might get caught with your head in the freezer! ❧

Not Mine

> The earth is the Lord's, and everything in it. The world and all its people belong to him.
>
> *Psalm 24:1*

Breast cancer tried to take everything away. Not just my breast, my hair, and my self-esteem. It tried to steal my dreams. Would I be around to plan my daughter's wedding or hold my first grandchild? Who would decorate my house for Christmas and plant my garden? Ten years from now, would I be the one riding on the back of our Gold Wing? What about all those plans we've made over a fresh cup of coffee and the morning newspaper? It wasn't just me who felt threatened. Cancer tried to steal my husband's wife, my children's mother, my parents' daughter, and my brother's sister. It rocked our world and everything in it.

Is it *our* world? King David was wealthy and successful when he acknowledged everything in heaven and earth belonged to God (1 Chronicles 29:11). He was amazed that the Lord would bless him so extravagantly (1 Chronicles 17:16). David praised God for the people's generous offerings to build the Temple of his God saying: "It all belongs to you!" (1 Chronicles 29:16). God himself described David as a man after God's own heart (1 Samuel 13:14; Acts 13:22). Even in the dark times when he stumbled and fell into sin, David had a wholehearted unwavering devotion to God. His heart was humble and filled with gratitude. He never took God's mercy lightly or His blessings for granted.

We too have been richly blessed: families we love, comfortable homes, good health care, plenty to eat, and freedom to do as we please. Perhaps like me, you fear this cancer will rob you of everything. Good news! The Lord has awesome plans for you. He *wants* to prosper you, not harm you. He *wants* to give you hope and a future (Jeremiah 29:11). He wants to bless you just as He blessed David. He wants your relationship with Him to be the center of your life. He wants no material thing, no earthly relationship, not even life itself, to be more important than His incredible love for you (Luke 14:26–27, 33; Philippians 3:7–8). Praise God, the source of all your blessings! The earth and everything in it is His. Not yours. Not mine. Only His. ❦

RESCUE ME!

BUT NOW, O ISRAEL, THE LORD WHO
CREATED YOU SAYS: "DO NOT BE AFRAID,
FOR I HAVE RANSOMED YOU. I HAVE CALLED
YOU BY NAME; YOU ARE MINE. WHEN YOU
GO THROUGH DEEP WATERS AND GREAT
TROUBLE, I WILL BE WITH YOU. WHEN YOU
GO THROUGH RIVERS OF DIFFICULTY, YOU
WILL NOT DROWN! WHEN YOU WALK
THROUGH THE FIRE OF OPPRESSION, YOU
WILL NOT BE BURNED UP; THE FLAMES WILL
NOT CONSUME YOU. FOR I AM THE LORD,
YOUR GOD, THE HOLY ONE OF ISRAEL,
YOUR SAVIOR."

Isaiah 43:1–3

Even after my biopsy was positive, I still held on to hope. My doctor was optimistic. She found no clinical evidence of lymph node involvement and the tumor was small. With negative nodes I would only need a lumpectomy and six weeks of radiation. No chemo and a better prognosis. Up until the day of the surgery, we prayed and prayed for negative nodes. I believed our prayers were answered right up until the minute I started counting backwards on the operating table and drifted off to sleep. I awoke to devastating news . . . two positive sentinel nodes and twenty-four weeks of chemotherapy. The deep waters of trouble just got deeper.

I wanted so badly for God to snatch me out of the fire and rescue me from my trouble. I had prepared myself for stage 1 cancer. Lymph node involvement and chemotherapy took my cancer to a different level. Now I had to walk *through* the fire. Sometimes God reaches right down from heaven and pulls us out of the deep waters (Psalm 18:16). Other times, He holds us up and keeps us from drowning (Psalm 18:18). Either way, He promises to rescue us from each and every trouble we face. He always hears our cry for help and He is always at our side (Psalm 34:17–20). When the waters of my cancer got deeper, I was weak and powerless on my own. But God upheld me. He didn't let me drown. And all I had to do was ask.

If you invite the Lord into the fire of your cancer, the flames will not consume you. After all, your God is in the rescue business. He's been doing it for four thousand years. It was God who rescued the Israelites from slavery (Exodus 20:2). He rescued them repeatedly when they cried out for help (Nehemiah 9:28). He rescued David from his enemies (2 Samuel 22:17–18). He rescued Job from his suffering (Job 42:10). He rescued Shadrach, Meshach, and Abednego from the fiery furnace (Daniel 3). He rescued Daniel from the lions (Daniel 6:19–21). Then He pulled off the greatest rescue mission of all time. He sent His Son to die on a cross. He conquered death so you can have life. He ransomed you! He knows you by name. You *belong* to Him. So you can be sure when His very own child walks through the fire of breast cancer, you will not be burned up. All you have to do is call on your Savior. *Rescue me!* ❦

BEAUTY QUEEN

> DON'T BE CONCERNED ABOUT THE
> OUTWARD BEAUTY THAT DEPENDS ON
> FANCY HAIRSTYLES, EXPENSIVE JEWELRY, OR
> BEAUTIFUL CLOTHES. YOU SHOULD BE
> KNOWN FOR THE BEAUTY THAT COMES
> FROM WITHIN, THE UNFADING BEAUTY OF A
> GENTLE AND QUIET SPIRIT, WHICH IS SO
> PRECIOUS TO GOD.
>
> *1 Peter 3:3–4*

*Look Good. . . . Feel Better.*sm Sign me up! The class was sponsored by the American Cancer Society and my cancer clinic. It promised to teach me beauty techniques that would enhance my appearance and self-image so I could cope with "unpleasant side effects" of cancer treatment. Now that should be a challenge! About fifteen women attended. Some were already hairless, and others would be soon. We practiced applying makeup and painting on fake eyebrows. We learned tricks for fooling people into thinking we still had eyelashes. We learned how to style our wigs and tips to keep them from falling off our heads. I walked out of the class with a bag of goodies . . . lotions and potions for dry skin, assorted cosmetics, and coupons for wig shops and beauty supplies. I was looking good and feeling better already.

One day about halfway through my chemo, I put on some perky workout clothes, applied all my makeup tricks, put on my cap with the hair fringe attached, and headed for the gym. I had this beauty thing down to a science. After my walk, I stood in front of the large wall mirror in the locker room. The beauty queen next to me with the perfectly toned body pulled off her cap and her long beautiful hair tumbled down onto her shoulders. She started fluffing it. She fluffed, admired, and fluffed some more. I was screaming inside. I was *so* tempted to whip off my hair cap, and "fluff" my bald head. If it weren't for the little girl standing next to me, I might have. I didn't want to scare her.

God, why do I feel this way? At that moment, all the beauty tips, even knowing my situation was temporary, didn't matter. Maybe it was because people had always commented on my thick black hair. It was my "best feature." And cancer stole it from me. Maybe God was trying to teach me something. Maybe I don't need the approval of others to feel good about myself (Galatians 1:10). Maybe I don't need to compare myself with others (Galatians 6:4). Just maybe, all I need is God. He loves me, and that's enough. He's not concerned about my beautiful skin. He's not concerned about my beautiful hair. He's concerned about the beauty inside my heart.

What a comfort to know God cares more about your inner beauty than your outward appearance. Your beautiful skin and hair will fade away. Cancer may steal it today. Age may steal it tomorrow. But true beauty comes from your inner character . . . a character that comes only from a deep devotion to God. Women known for such beauty will be greatly praised (Proverbs 31:30). The next time you apply all your makeup tricks, know that your true beauty rests deep inside you. It's the unfading beauty of your gentle spirit that is so precious to God. So start looking good and feeling better. In His eyes, you're a beauty queen.

WHEN YOU CAN'T PRAY

> AND THE HOLY SPIRIT HELPS US IN OUR
> DISTRESS. FOR WE DON'T EVEN KNOW WHAT
> WE SHOULD PRAY FOR, NOR HOW WE
> SHOULD PRAY. BUT THE HOLY SPIRIT PRAYS
> FOR US WITH GROANINGS THAT CANNOT BE
> EXPRESSED IN WORDS. AND THE FATHER
> WHO KNOWS ALL HEARTS KNOWS WHAT THE
> SPIRIT IS SAYING, FOR THE SPIRIT PLEADS
> FOR US BELIEVERS IN HARMONY WITH
> GOD'S OWN WILL.
> *Romans 8:26–27*

For three weeks I couldn't pray. From the day my doctor found the lump in my breast up until the day before the biopsy report, I was numb. Others prayed for me as I made my way to the hospital for a mammogram and an ultrasound. They kept praying when the results pointed me to the breast surgeon and the surgeon sent me back to the hospital for a needle core biopsy. The whole time, I couldn't pray. I watched myself from a distance, as though it was someone else living in my body going through all the motions. But I felt nothing. I felt dead inside. I tried and tried to cry out to God, but the words stuck in my throat.

All this time, God never left me to my own resources. The entire time I couldn't find the right words to pray, the Holy Spirit pleaded my case before my heavenly Father. God knows us intimately. He knows all hearts. He knows every need, every desire, every motive, and every thought (1 Chronicles 28:9). The Word says He answers our prayers even before we ask. While we are still struggling to know our needs, He has already started to answer our prayers (Isaiah 65:24). And that's exactly what He did. After the diagnosis was confirmed, the Lord sent me a new surgeon and a new procedure, and all the pieces fell perfectly into place. All the details surrounding the surgery were exactly what I would have prayed for . . . and I didn't even have to ask.

You can trust that the Father who knows all hearts knows your heart too. Right now, you might be so overwhelmed with grief and despair that your cries for help are stuck in your throat. You can take comfort in knowing that the Holy Spirit is pleading your case before your Father in heaven. Your Father knows every need and hears every request before you ask. If you trust Him completely and commit everything to Him, He promises to give you the desires of your heart (Psalm 37:4–5). When it all comes together—the skillful surgeon, the perfect timing, the help you need—you'll stand in amazement and wonder: *How did He know?* Because when you can't pray—when you don't know how or what to pray—even then your Father knows. ❦

SHOW ME YOUR POWER

"HOW LONG HAS THIS BEEN HAPPENING?"
JESUS ASKED THE BOY'S FATHER. HE REPLIED,
"SINCE HE WAS VERY SMALL. THE EVIL SPIRIT
OFTEN MAKES HIM FALL INTO THE FIRE OR
INTO WATER, TRYING TO KILL HIM. HAVE
MERCY ON US AND HELP US. DO SOMETHING
IF YOU CAN." "WHAT DO YOU MEAN, 'IF I
CAN'?" JESUS ASKED. "ANYTHING IS POSSIBLE
IF A PERSON BELIEVES." THE FATHER
INSTANTLY REPLIED, "I DO BELIEVE, BUT
HELP ME NOT TO DOUBT!"
Mark 9:21–24

*T*he candles flickered in the dimly lit chapel. Three prayer ministers laid hands on me and started to pray. They praised God for my healing. They thanked Him for upholding and protecting me through the months of chemotherapy. They prayed that His supernatural peace would continue to guard my heart against all anxiety. They affirmed the words of the prophet Isaiah that no weapon formed against me would prosper and the Lord would double my portion of prosperity and joy. *O Lord. I believe! I can't deny your presence in this place. Please, help me not to doubt.*

I'm not the first believer to doubt. There was the father who sought healing for his deaf and mute son. The disciples couldn't heal him. The father confessed his belief and immediately asked Jesus to increase his faith. Jesus responded by healing his son (Mark 9:17–29). Then there was Thomas. He wouldn't believe Jesus rose from the dead until he could put his fingers on the nail wounds and place his hand into the wound on Jesus' side. Jesus didn't condemn Thomas for doubting. He showed himself to Thomas and let him touch His wounds (John 20:25–27). Both Thomas and the father of the deaf and mute son *wanted* to believe. Doubt was only a temporary stop in their faith journey. It led them to seek Jesus, and anyone who seeks Him will be rewarded (Hebrews 11:6). Because they asked, the Lord showed His power. Their doubt led them to Christ.

Do you want proof? Do you want to know for certain that God is God and He will do what He promises? Do you want to see Jesus and hear His voice? Do you want evidence that He knows about your cancer and He hears your prayers? Don't let your doubt discourage you. The Lord is as close as your Bible. Its pages are filled with the testimony of countless believers who walked alongside Him and witnessed His power. The power of the living God is as close as your prayers. The Holy Spirit dwelling inside you is your direct line to your heavenly Father. Let your doubt carry you to the foot of the Cross. Seek Him with all your heart. Ask Him to increase your faith. *Lord, help me not to doubt. Show me your power!* He'll start showing you things you never dreamed possible. *

REST FOR YOUR SOUL

> THEN JESUS SAID, "COME TO ME, ALL OF
> YOU WHO ARE WEARY AND CARRY HEAVY
> BURDENS, AND I WILL GIVE YOU REST. TAKE
> MY YOKE UPON YOU. LET ME TEACH YOU,
> BECAUSE I AM HUMBLE AND GENTLE, AND
> YOU WILL FIND REST FOR YOUR SOULS. FOR
> MY YOKE FITS PERFECTLY, AND THE BURDEN
> I GIVE YOU IS LIGHT."
> *Matthew 11:28–30*

In the beginning I took it with me everywhere. I dragged it down the steps in the morning and up the steps to my bedroom at night. I heaved it onto the bed and slept with it. I dragged it to church on Sundays and to my client meetings on Monday morning. I dragged it through parking lots, up and down elevators, and to my daughter's dance competitions. I lugged it back and forth to the doctor's office and the hospital. With each test result, it got heavier and heavier. The thought of what breast cancer might do to me and my family was overwhelming. The burden was becoming more than I could bear. I was exhausted from dragging it around. Then I heard the Lord whisper. *You don't have to carry it, you know. I can take it from you. Come to me and I will give you rest.*

Jesus took the burden of my cancer on himself. He took every worry, every fear, everything that weighed me down. He offered me God's ultimate rest . . . a peace found only in a personal relationship with Christ . . . a peace not of this world (John 14:27). God prepared a place of rest for the Israelites too. He rescued them from four hundred years of slavery and promised to give them the land of Canaan. But they disobeyed God's command to conquer the land and refused to believe in His protection. God eventually allowed Joshua and Caleb to enter the Promised Land because they were faithful. The others wandered in the desert for forty years and never entered His place of rest (Numbers 14; Psalm 95:7–11; Hebrews 3:16–19).

How heavy is your burden today? Are you tired of dragging it with you wherever you go? I have good news! God prepared you a place of rest and all who believe can enter it (Hebrews 4:1–3). Every day, the difficulty of your cancer will try to steal His promise. Don't be fooled like the Israelites. Trust the Lord and enter your Promised Land. He can protect you through the valley of your cancer and lead you safely to the other side. Lay your burden at His feet. Let Him lighten your load. Enter His place of rest where the meadows are green and the healing waters flow (Psalm 23:2). You don't have to wait until the next life to find rest for your soul. You can have it now. ❦

COME AND DRINK

> AS THE DEER PANTS FOR STREAMS OF
> WATER, SO I LONG FOR YOU, O GOD. I
> THIRST FOR GOD, THE LIVING GOD. WHEN
> CAN I COME AND STAND BEFORE HIM?
> *Psalm 42:1–2*

I was always a perfectionist. At four, I colored every page in my Cinderella color book in order from the beginning, and I never colored outside the lines. From dolls and books to clothes and schoolwork, my childhood was all about perfection. As I grew older, my perfectionism produced college degrees, prestigious jobs, and personal accomplishments. If we left our perfectly decorated house to go camping, we had to find the perfect campsite. If we went on vacation, we had to have perfect accommodations and perfect weather. I wanted my kids to have perfect birthday parties and perfect holidays. Breast cancer didn't fit into my perfect plan. It was messy, ugly, unpredictable, and out of my control. I couldn't tackle it like a work project or a Christmas dinner. I couldn't fall back on good impressions or my list of accomplishments to fill the empty pit it left in my soul. Even the perfect doctors I found couldn't satisfy my deepest need.

Only God can satisfy. He gave each of us a great big God-sized hole inside that only He can fill. It was part of His plan for us to live in fellowship with Him, so He hardwired it right into our DNA. The psalmist compared this deep longing for God to a deer whose life depends on water. King David's very soul thirsted for God. Stripped of all his possessions and hiding from his enemies in the barren wilderness, he cried, "My whole body longs for you in this parched and weary land where there is no water" (Psalm 63:1). For a long time, I tried to win approval and accumulate achievements to satisfy my thirst for God. Others might strive to accumulate money, power, or material possessions. Until our world crashes, we often try to fill our God-sized hole with everything but God.

As you and your doctors battle your cancer, modern medicine will give you the best it has to offer. Do you still have an empty pit in your soul? Maybe you thirst for something more. God wants to give you a different kind of water. He wants to give you living water to quench your thirsty soul (John 4:10). He wants to give you Jesus, the fountain of life (Psalm 36:9). Jesus is the gift that satisfies your soul's desire. The living Christ within you can quench your thirst for God forever. And when everything else falls short, when the world around you proves it isn't perfect, that God-sized hole in your heart will be filled to overflowing. He's more than enough. He's all you need. So come and drink! (Isaiah 55:1). You'll never be thirsty again. ❦

BIBLE THUMPER

> THEY WERE DEEPLY OFFENDED AND REFUSED
> TO BELIEVE IN HIM. THEN JESUS TOLD THEM,
> "A PROPHET IS HONORED EVERYWHERE
> EXCEPT IN HIS OWN HOMETOWN AND
> AMONG HIS RELATIVES AND HIS OWN
> FAMILY." AND BECAUSE OF THEIR UNBELIEF,
> HE COULDN'T DO ANY MIGHTY MIRACLES
> AMONG THEM EXCEPT TO PLACE HIS HANDS
> ON A FEW SICK PEOPLE AND HEAL THEM.
> AND HE WAS AMAZED AT THEIR UNBELIEF.
> *Mark 6:3b–6a*

I used to call them "Bible thumpers." They carried their Bibles to church every Sunday in little zippered covers. Each book had a tab so they could quickly locate the passages. All the pages were underlined and marked up with notes. They would talk openly about their relationship with Jesus and other religious matters that were best kept in private. It just wasn't normal conversation. Every week our pastors encouraged me to become one of them. Bring your Bible! If you didn't bring one, the ushers will give you one. Take it home. Read it every day. Join a small group of other Christians who will hold you accountable for your faith journey. For a long time, I refused to bring my Bible or take one from the ushers. I took offense. *Who do these people think they are, being so religious and trying to tell me what to do?* Maybe I took offense because it brought me closer to a decision point. *Is Jesus the leader of my life or isn't He?* Maybe I was afraid . . . afraid of what God might do, or worse yet, what He might require of me.

God used breast cancer to get my attention. I started taking the Bible when the usher offered it to me. Eventually I bought my own . . . with a little zippered cover. I even started underlining. As I read more and more, I learned that my offense came with a price. Jesus couldn't do mighty miracles in His own hometown because the people refused to believe and were deeply offended by Him.

But He healed a Gentile woman's daughter simply because she refused to take offense. As she pleaded her case, Jesus tested her: "It isn't right to take food from the children and throw it to the dogs." She could have been offended. He called her a dog! Instead, she said she would settle for the crumbs from His table. He blessed her instantly (Matthew 15:21–28).

Fear can also separate us from God's blessing. Jesus sent demons out of a sick man into a herd of two thousand pigs that plunged over a steep bank into the lake. The crowd watching begged Him to go away and leave them alone (Mark 5:1–17). His supernatural power terrified them. They were afraid of what it might cost to follow Him.

Maybe this cancer is bringing you closer to a decision point. Maybe you're afraid of what the Lord might require of you. As you seek God to restore your health, you can trust He has awesome plans for your life (John 10:10). There is a room full of blessings with your name on it . . . one glorious blessing after another (John 1:16). "You could dabble in your faith. But if you give Him everything you've got, He'll give you fullness of life and then some" (Ephesians 3:19–20). He'll open the floodgates and pour out every spiritual blessing in the heavenly realm (Ephesians 1:3–5). So don't let offense or fear steal your blessing. Dig deep into the Word. Open it, underline it, or carry it in a little zippered cover. Before long, you'll be thumping your Bible with the best of them. ❦

BUMPER CROP

THE RAIN AND SNOW COME DOWN FROM
THE HEAVENS AND STAY ON THE GROUND
TO WATER THE EARTH. THEY CAUSE THE
GRAIN TO GROW, PRODUCING SEED FOR THE
FARMER AND BREAD FOR THE HUNGRY. IT IS
THE SAME WITH MY WORD. I SEND IT OUT,
AND IT ALWAYS PRODUCES FRUIT. IT WILL
ACCOMPLISH ALL I WANT IT TO, AND IT WILL
PROSPER EVERYWHERE I SEND IT. YOU WILL
LIVE IN JOY AND PEACE. THE MOUNTAINS
AND HILLS WILL BURST INTO SONG, AND THE
TREES OF THE FIELD WILL CLAP THEIR
HANDS! WHERE ONCE THERE WERE
THORNS, CYPRESS TREES WILL GROW.
WHERE BRIERS GREW, MYRTLES WILL
SPROUT UP.

Isaiah 55:10–13

I drove my family crazy with my pocket-sized magnifying glass. Every night before bed I held it up to my bald head and leaned up close to the bathroom mirror, squinting to see if any hairs were sprouting. I saw nothing but hairless follicles. Discouraged, I handed the magnifying glass to my husband and asked him to look. After all, he had better eyesight. When he failed to locate any sign of new growth, I would make my way to my daughter's room and ask her to look. Night after night, I waited for the first tiny hairs to appear. Night after night, they confirmed what I already knew. Nothing. Finally, my husband started telling me what I wanted to hear . . . *I think I see something!* I could tell by the gentle smile on his face he was teasing. The bantering went on for weeks. Here she comes again with the magnifying glass!

It seemed like an eternity before the first hairs peeked out of my barren little follicles. Isn't it the same with God? We grow impatient when He seems slow to answer our prayers or His promises take forever to materialize. But His Word never comes back empty. Just as rain and snow come down from heaven to water the farmer's field and produce crops, God's Word always produces fruit. Sometimes the fruit doesn't come as quickly as we'd like. My treatment and recovery seemed to go on forever, but God didn't waste His time or mine. He revealed more of himself to me, taught me patience, and strengthened my character (James 1:2–4; Romans 5:3–4). He never left my side (Hebrews 13:5). He used my suffering for my good and His glory (2 Thessalonians 1:4–6). He came into my heart so I could speak to yours. Our God never has a crop failure. Sooner or later, His Word *always* produces fruit.

In this world of instant gratification, we want results and we want them now! You can take comfort in knowing God doesn't make promises He won't keep. Sometimes things take longer than we expect, but His timing is always perfect (Romans 8:25). Eventually the chemo will end, the hair will grow back, and life will return to normal. The words you prayed and the Scripture you spoke will come down like rain from heaven, watering the earth and producing fruit. The mountains and hills will burst into song, and the trees of the field will clap their hands! Where once there was despair, hope will grow. Where nothing grew, tiny hairs will sprout up. Get out the magnifying glass. It's a bumper crop! 🌾

PLANTING IN TEARS

RESTORE OUR FORTUNES, LORD, AS
STREAMS RENEW THE DESERT. THOSE WHO
PLANT IN TEARS WILL HARVEST WITH
SHOUTS OF JOY. THEY WEEP AS THEY GO TO
PLANT THEIR SEED, BUT THEY SING AS THEY
RETURN WITH THE HARVEST.

Psalm 126:4–6

Four couples planned the trip for months. We called our-selves the Kalifornia Kids. We dreamed of winding through the mountains on our way west and letting the sheer beauty of glacier-clad peaks and plunging valleys take our breath away. Images of alpine meadows, thick forests of hemlocks and cedars, and waterfalls cascading over cliffs into pristine blue lakes filled our imaginations. My husband called it "eye candy." However, as our motorcycles slowly meandered through Going-to-the-Sun Road in Glacier National Park, the smoky haze in the air grew thicker and it became more difficult to breathe. The panoramic views dis-appointed as thick black clouds of smoke rose from patches of burning forest and filled the once-blue sky. In other areas of the park, baby pines and green vegetation were making a comeback under the charred skeletons of trees from a fire several years earlier.

I didn't envision breast cancer any more than I envisioned for-est fires in Glacier National Park. But God's amazing ability to restore life was evident in both situations. He can restore a forest after a devastating fire. He can restore health after cancer. He is able to bring good out of any tragedy. Our human tendency is to despair and fall into self-pity in times of crisis. But the psalmist says if we plant seed during this time of weeping, our tears of sadness can turn into a harvest of joy. If we press into God and reach out to bless others in the midst of our grief, we will receive fruit from the seed we plant. During my darkest times, I found an unexplained comfort in reaching out to others who were suffering. God promises if we don't get discouraged but plant to please Him, we will reap a harvest of blessing in due time (Galatians 6:9).

Your cancer is not a permanent condition—although right now that may be difficult to believe. And your God is a restoration expert. For hundreds of years, He promised through the prophets to restore His fallen kingdom (Amos 9:11). He fulfilled the promise in Christ's resurrection (Acts 15:16–17). He removed your sin and restored you to himself. As a believer, you have been declared righteous so you can know and experience His love and His plan for you (Romans 4:24).

Right now, you may doubt both His love and His plan. Your suffering may feel as though it will never end. Deep inside you may feel barren and lifeless, like a forest after a devastating fire. But God promises it will only last a little while (1 Peter 5:10). Very soon, the charred wasteland inside your heart will come to life again. If you trust Him, God will bring more fruit from your cancer than you can imagine. Plant in tears! You'll be singing for joy when your harvest comes! ✾

What . . . Me Worry?

> DON'T WORRY ABOUT ANYTHING; INSTEAD,
> PRAY ABOUT EVERYTHING. TELL GOD WHAT
> YOU NEED, AND THANK HIM FOR ALL HE HAS
> DONE. IF YOU DO THIS, YOU WILL
> EXPERIENCE GOD'S PEACE, WHICH IS FAR
> MORE WONDERFUL THAN THE HUMAN MIND
> CAN UNDERSTAND. HIS PEACE WILL GUARD
> YOUR HEARTS AND MINDS AS YOU LIVE
> IN CHRIST JESUS.
> *Philippians 4:6–7*

If you're prone to chronic worry, breast cancer will either push you over the edge or cure you altogether. It sure gave me plenty of "what ifs" to add to my worry list. What if the surgeon didn't get all the cancer? What if I get lymphedema? What if my nodes are positive and I have to have chemo? What if the chemo doesn't work? What if I have cancer in the other breast too? Shouldn't they do an ultrasound to be sure? What if something shows up on the chest X ray? What if this backache is something more than a backache? What if people can tell I'm wearing a wig? What if my hair grows back gray or curly or thin, or doesn't come back at all?

The list goes on and on. From the day of my diagnosis, I could spend the rest of my life waiting for the other shoe to drop. Or I could trust Jesus. He has plenty to say about worry. *Listen, I'm the Creator of the universe. . . . Don't you think you can trust me with the details of your life? Can all these worries change your situation one little bit? No. It's more harmful to your health than helpful. Do you think for one minute I ignore those who depend on me? I care for birds and flowers. Wouldn't I care more for you? I already know all your needs. Don't you trust me? If you keep worrying about all the details, you won't be available for the really important things I have planned for you. Just take it one day at a time* (Matthew 6:25–34).

Thank you, Lord. I need a reminder sometimes. Maybe you do too. Jesus tells us not to worry about the things God promises He will supply. When we worry we are consumed by fear and find it difficult to trust God. Worry can damage your health, disrupt your life, and steal your joy. What a relief to know you can give all your worries and cares to God. He cares about what happens to you (1 Peter 5:7). You don't have to worry about one little thing. Whenever you're tempted, turn your worries into prayers. *God, I refuse to worry about that test. It's your problem now.* Pray about every detail of your cancer and every detail of your life. Tell God what you need, and thank Him for all He has done. He will give you the peace that surpasses all human understanding. His supernatural peace will guard your heart against all anxiety. What . . . me worry? Not anymore! ❧

THIS IS YOUR CAPTAIN SPEAKING

> MY SHEEP RECOGNIZE MY VOICE; I KNOW
> THEM, AND THEY FOLLOW ME.
> *John 10:27*

*D*o you do much air travel? If so, then you know what I'm talking about. Before every flight departure, the flight attendants drone on about oxygen masks and emergency procedures. We've heard it all before so we tend to tune them out. But the moment there is significant turbulence, an unexplained route change, or a delay in takeoff or landing, we wait expectantly to hear the captain's voice from the cockpit. We want to know what's going on and we want to hear it from the voice of authority. When the voice finally announces, "Ladies and gentlemen, this is your captain speaking," we don't tune it out. We listen closely for an explanation and we're relieved to know the situation is under control.

Just like we wait for the flight captain's voice to calm our fears in times of trouble, we want to hear the voice of our true Captain, our heavenly Father. God doesn't speak to most of us in an audible voice like He spoke to Moses from a burning bush or to the apostle Paul from a brilliant light. When the Lord spoke to Elijah, He didn't speak through a mighty windstorm, an earthquake, or a fire. He spoke in a quiet whisper into Elijah's humbled heart (1 Kings 19:11–12). He usually speaks to us through this same quiet whisper. When we humble ourselves before God in prayer the Holy Spirit inside us speaks to our own spirit, our spirit speaks His message to our mind, and our mind knows what to do. Often during my cancer, the quiet whisper of God was my only guide. I felt inner peace when I decided to change surgeons and have a lumpectomy instead of a mastectomy. I knew which chemo regimen and hormone therapy to take because my spirit felt peaceful instead of uneasy.

God also speaks to us through His Word. For some, the Bible is merely a book of literature. But when the Holy Spirit dwells within us, the words come to life and get very personal. Countless times during my daily Bible study, the answer to a prayer or the solution to a current problem jumps off the page. This shouldn't be surprising. All Scripture is God-inspired and teaches us what is right. It's God's way to prepare and equip us for everything He wants us to do (2 Timothy 4:16–17).

Are you struggling to hear the voice of God? Keep praying and keep your Bible open. You're bound to recognize His voice. The next time your spirit prompts you to do something, don't delay! The more you obey His quiet whisper, the more He will speak to you, and the clearer His voice will become. Sooner or later, His peace will rule in your heart and guide all your decisions (Colossians 3:15). Listen! He's got an announcement to make. *Daughter, this is your Captain speaking.* What a relief! The Captain has your situation completely under control! ❦

FRUITFUL IN THE LAND OF YOUR SUFFERING

> OH, THE JOYS OF THOSE WHO DO NOT
> FOLLOW THE ADVICE OF THE WICKED, OR
> STAND AROUND WITH SINNERS, OR JOIN IN
> WITH SCOFFERS. BUT THEY DELIGHT IN
> DOING EVERYTHING THE LORD WANTS; DAY
> AND NIGHT THEY THINK ABOUT HIS LAW.
> THEY ARE LIKE TREES PLANTED ALONG THE
> RIVERBANK, BEARING FRUIT EACH SEASON
> WITHOUT FAIL. THEIR LEAVES NEVER
> WITHER, AND IN ALL THEY DO,
> THEY PROSPER.
> *Psalm 1:1–3*

*B*efore my diagnosis I didn't truly prosper. Oh, I was successful by the world's standards. I had a wonderful family, a nice house, a decent income, and no criminal record. But my thoughts and attitudes were shaped more by the world's view than God's. *I'm a reasonably intelligent woman. If I work hard, follow the rules, and watch my back, things will go my way.* When the small voice of my conscience told me to make peace with a neighbor or do something for God that was not on my busy schedule, I usually found an excuse. Cancer changed me. Cancer taught me the joy of obedience. It taught me to focus on Him and meditate on His Word. When we let God influence our thoughts and attitudes instead of a world that ridicules Him, we are blessed like healthy trees planted along a riverbank. We bear fruit every season without fail. If cancer comes and the world tells us our future is uncertain, even then our leaves never wither. Now that's prosperity.

Joseph understood obedience. He was so hated by his brothers that they sold him into slavery at the age of seventeen. Throughout his thirteen years as a slave and prisoner, he developed strong character and deep wisdom. His personal integrity and spiritual ability to interpret dreams won the respect and admiration of the Pharaoh, who made Joseph the second in command of all Egypt when he was only thirty years old. God used the evil actions of Joseph's brothers to fulfill His ultimate plan. As ruler, Joseph controlled the food supply that saved his brothers and Egypt from famine and paved the way for the nation of Israel (Genesis 37–50). Whether he was in the pit of despair or ruler of the land, Joseph faithfully obeyed God. God honored his faithfulness and made him fruitful in the land of his suffering (Genesis 41:52).

Just as a tree soaks up water and bears luscious fruit, you can soak up God's Word and produce actions and attitudes that honor God. Don't look for Him in the opinions of doubters or the thoughts of the world—you won't find Him there. As you meditate day and night on the words you read in the Bible, watch how He gives opportunities to apply His wisdom in your breast cancer journey. Right now, He's using your cancer to fulfill some master plan you can't even comprehend. People will come to sit under your shade and eat your fruit. They will seek you and draw encouragement from you because they see how God has blessed you in the land of your suffering. ☙

MAKE YOUR PEACE

LISTEN TO ME! YOU CAN PRAY FOR
ANYTHING, AND IF YOU BELIEVE, YOU WILL
HAVE IT. BUT WHEN YOU ARE PRAYING,
FIRST FORGIVE ANYONE YOU ARE HOLDING
A GRUDGE AGAINST, SO THAT YOUR FATHER
IN HEAVEN WILL FORGIVE YOUR SINS, TOO.
Mark 11:24–25

We all have people in our lives who have said and done things that hurt us deeply. When we live or work in close quarters with the offender, we may constantly battle anger and bitterness. Sometimes the hurt turns into an outward conflict. Or we might just hold it inside to avoid confrontation. For years, we might set aside the offense until a phone call, family gathering, or social event brings it all back again. We replay the tape over and over in our heads to justify our hurt and keep our bitterness alive. Each time we push the rewind button we are offended again. We can carry our hurt around with us for years. But who suffers most? Some say bitterness is like drinking poison and expecting the other person to die.

Jesus says we can pray for anything and receive it if we believe. But He also warns that broken relationships and unforgiveness hinder our prayers. Unresolved anger against another person violates God's command to love. It can be a dangerous emotion leading to hostility, mental stress, and spiritual damage. It can steal our joy and stand in the way of our relationship with God. We can hardly plead our case to God in prayer and claim to love Him while we feel a deep resentment toward someone. Jesus tells us to go and be reconciled to that person before we come before Him (Matthew 5:22–24). He tells us to love and pray for that person. Then, He really drives the point home: "If you love only those who love you, what good is that?" (Matthew 5:44–46).

Ouch. I know exactly what you're thinking. I've been there. *But, you don't know what they did to me. God, sometimes you just ask too much of me.* The Lord knows what they did to you. And He feels your hurt. He is no stranger to your pain. With His dying breath, He pleaded with God to forgive those who whipped Him, spat on Him, and nailed Him to the cross. He is our ultimate role model for unconditional love. God knows you can't make yourself *feel* love and forgiveness for those who hurt you. But He can. The Holy Spirit within you will *show* love when you feel no love. When we let Him love our enemies through us, we show that Jesus is truly Lord of our life.

The next time you bring your cancer before God, first ask Him to renew a right spirit within you (Psalm 51:10–13). Ask Him to forgive you and cleanse you of any resentment or bitterness hidden in your heart (Ephesians 4:31). Ask Him to help you forgive that person you are holding a grudge against and to restore your broken relationship (Colossians 3:13). Don't let unforgiveness hinder your prayers. Ask Him to heal your body, your soul, *and* your spirit. It's time to make your peace. ❦

HANG ON TO YOUR SEAT

WHEN I THINK OF THE WISDOM AND SCOPE
OF GOD'S PLAN, I FALL TO MY KNEES AND
PRAY TO THE FATHER, THE CREATOR OF
EVERYTHING IN HEAVEN AND ON EARTH. I
PRAY THAT FROM HIS GLORIOUS, UNLIMITED
RESOURCES HE WILL GIVE YOU MIGHTY
INNER STRENGTH THROUGH HIS HOLY
SPIRIT. AND I PRAY THAT CHRIST WILL BE
MORE AND MORE AT HOME IN YOUR
HEARTS AS YOU TRUST IN HIM. MAY YOUR
ROOTS GO DOWN DEEP INTO THE SOIL OF
GOD'S MARVELOUS LOVE. AND MAY YOU
HAVE THE POWER TO UNDERSTAND, AS ALL
GOD'S PEOPLE SHOULD, HOW WIDE, HOW
LONG, HOW HIGH, AND HOW DEEP HIS LOVE
REALLY IS. MAY YOU EXPERIENCE THE LOVE
OF CHRIST, THOUGH IT IS SO GREAT YOU
WILL NEVER FULLY UNDERSTAND IT. THEN
YOU WILL BE FILLED WITH THE FULLNESS OF
LIFE AND POWER THAT COMES FROM GOD.
Ephesians 3:14–19

I thought my life was full and complete. I had a strong faith in God. I went to church almost every Sunday. My kids were baptized and confirmed. I even did a little volunteer work when it fit into my schedule. I knew God was always there for me in times of crisis. I thought of myself as a mature Christian. In my pride, I thought I understood everything He had to show me. Then I got breast cancer. Never in my wildest dreams did I think something like this would ever happen to me. In the months that followed, I learned I had barely scratched the surface in my understanding of God and His power. I had been living in a black-and-white world. God wanted to show me living color.

God showed me the wisdom and scope of His plan. His Son died so I can live an abundant life in my Father's presence. He showed me that the Creator of everything in heaven and on earth has authority over my breast cancer and everyone involved in my treatment. He gave me a taste of His unlimited resources through a mighty inner strength that surpassed all human understanding. The more I trusted Him and spent time with Him in prayer and Bible study, the more at home He became in my heart, and the more I could recognize His voice over all the others. As my roots grew down into the soil of His love, He showed me it was big enough to reach every corner of my life. It was wide enough to cover every detail of my breast cancer. It was long enough to cover my life afterward. His love reached the heights of my good times and the depths of my despair.

What do you suppose God wants to show you? Imagine your treatment is over and you're going out to celebrate at a wonderful new restaurant. You get all dressed up and climb into your brand-new sports car, but to your dismay, the car is stuck in first gear. You creep along slowly and finally arrive at the restaurant. By this time, you're starving. The waiter seats you and you open the menu with great anticipation. You are quickly disappointed. There's only one item to choose from—meatloaf. Without Christ in the center, your life is a little like this disappointing night on the town. You will never get out of first gear. You will never fully experience His power. There will never be anything but meatloaf on the menu. The fullness of life can only be experienced when you are united with Jesus (Colossians 2:9). Let your roots go down deep into the soil of His love. Seek Him with all your heart and trust Him with your cancer. Then hang on to your seat! He wants to show you everything He's got. ❦

YOU CAN'T HIDE

AND SOLOMON, MY SON, GET TO KNOW THE
GOD OF YOUR ANCESTORS. WORSHIP AND
SERVE HIM WITH YOUR WHOLE HEART AND
WITH A WILLING MIND. FOR THE LORD SEES
EVERY HEART AND UNDERSTANDS AND
KNOWS EVERY PLAN AND THOUGHT. IF YOU
SEEK HIM, YOU WILL FIND HIM.
1 Chronicles 28:9

It makes no sense to try to hide your thoughts and actions from
your all-knowing Father. Believe me, I've tried. God, do you
really know about the times I put my offering in the plate and
secretly wished I could spend it on something else? How about
when I do something for you but try to take the glory for myself?
Or when I try to please others instead of you? What about the
times I've stretched the truth a little to make things go my way?
How about when I've been angry with you because I couldn't
understand your plan? And what about the time when I. . . ? *Yes,
I know it all.* Wow. God knows my deepest, darkest secrets—the
worst things about me—and loves me anyway. Now that's
grace . . . unmerited, undeserved favor from my heavenly Father.

King David learned he could hide nothing from God. David
wholeheartedly sought Him. Yet he fell into sin. He committed
adultery with Bathsheba and then had her husband killed in an
attempt to cover it up. He repented and God forgave him, but He
did not spare David some of the consequences of his sin (2 Samuel
11–12). David counseled his son Solomon to seek God, who
knows every thought and every plan. In spite of all the things He

knows about us, from the blatant sin to the hidden motives in our hearts, God loves us. He wants to give us a hope and a future. He wants to restore us to himself. All He asks is that we seek Him with a whole and willing heart (Jeremiah 29:11–14). He promises to stay with us as long as we stay with Him (2 Chronicles 15:2). By the death and resurrection of Christ, He wiped our slate clean. When we repent, He not only forgives our wrongdoings. He never remembers them again (Hebrews 9:12). Our sin is as far removed as the east is from the west (Psalm 103:12).

God's intimate knowledge of you is no cause for alarm. He has already examined your heart and knows everything about you. You can't sit down or stand up without Him knowing. He knows your every thought. He knows what you're going to say before you say it. You can never escape from His Spirit (Psalm 139:1–7). He was with you on the day you were formed and He was with you on the day your cancer was diagnosed. He is with you now and He is with you always (Romans 8:28). He knows everything and loves you anyway! Right now, He is loving you, guiding you, and protecting you through every step of your cancer treatment. There's simply no escape from His comforting presence. You can run, but you can't hide. Why would you want to? ❦

River of Healing

> Everything that touches the water of this river will live. Fish will abound in the Dead Sea, for its waters will be healed. Wherever this water flows, everything will live. . . . All kinds of fruit trees will grow along both sides of the river. The leaves of these trees will never turn brown and fall, and there will always be fruit on their branches. There will be a new crop every month, without fail! For they are watered by the river flowing from the Temple. The fruit will be for food and the leaves for healing.
>
> *Ezekiel 47:9, 12*

Ezekiel served as a priest and prophet during Israel's seventy-year captivity in Babylon. He was obedient to God and fearlessly preached God's Word to the exiled Jews in the streets. He prophesied the fall of Jerusalem to a stubborn, unbelieving people, but He also consoled them by promising a day when God would pour out His spirit and restore all those who turn from sin. The people had just seen their nation and its temple destroyed with no hope of rebuilding in the near future when an angel gave Ezekiel a vision of a new temple. It was a message of hope and complete restoration at a time when they had no hope (Ezekiel 40–43).

The new temple symbolized God's perfect plan for His people. Woven in Ezekiel's description of the temple was the importance of worshiping God, the presence of the Lord in our hearts, and the blessings that flow from making Him the center of our lives. The river of healing that flowed from the temple was a sign that all life comes directly from God. The river flowed into the Dead Sea where the water is so salty it can't support life (Ezekiel 47:8). But the river purified and restored life to the Dead Sea. The trees on both sides of the river always bore fruit and the leaves never turned brown. The river restored life, just as God can restore us. In the midst of our sickness and despair, when life is beyond all hope, His power can heal.

God may have sent this message of hope 2,500 years ago to the captives in Babylonia, but the same message stands today. He is holy and righteous. He never changes (Malachi 3:6). His message to you has been the same since the beginning of time. Even when He allowed the nation of Israel to be destroyed for their disobedience, He still gave the people hope. God will restore all who remain faithful to Him. In the brokenness of your cancer, in the depths of your pain, He has not forgotten you. He never forgets those who faithfully seek Him in the midst of their suffering. Close your eyes right now. Go stand right in the middle of that river. Jump in it, dance in it, splash in it . . . lie down and soak in it. Let the healing waters wash over you and restore health to your body and life to your soul. Then step out into the glorious future He has planned for you! ❦

BE LIKE JESUS

> AND ALL OF US HAVE HAD THAT VEIL
> REMOVED SO THAT WE CAN BE MIRRORS
> THAT BRIGHTLY REFLECT THE GLORY OF
> THE LORD. AND AS THE SPIRIT OF THE
> LORD WORKS WITHIN US, WE BECOME MORE
> AND MORE LIKE HIM AND REFLECT HIS
> GLORY EVEN MORE.
> *2 Corinthians 3:18*

I remember when every kid across the country wanted to "be like Mike." All they had to do was wear the right shoes and they could slam dunk just like basketball superstar Michael Jordan. The ad campaign was a marketing genius and became the mantra for basketball followers and anyone wanting to look cool. As Christ's followers, we have our own mantra: Be like Jesus. The problem is, it's not a slam dunk! The apostle Paul compared the process of becoming more like Christ to the grueling preparation of an athlete in training (1 Corinthians 9:24–27, Philippians 3:12–14). Maybe that's why we don't see more Christians radiating the light of Jesus everywhere we go.

To be honest, I didn't think much about becoming more and more like Jesus. It wasn't until I was bald and broken that the Lord could really start doing His transforming work in me. It was my brokenness that led me to read God's Word, study the life of Jesus in the Gospels, and spend time with God in prayer. As my knowledge deepened, His truth started transforming me. The Holy Spirit started changing me from the inside out. For a long time, I had this backward. I thought I had to do the changing before I was worthy of being in a relationship with God. Now I know He does the work inside my heart. All I have to do is make myself available and be obedient to Him.

Spiritual maturity is not about how much we know or how much Scripture we can recite. It's not about how many church committees we serve on or how many Bible studies we participate in. It's not even about how many hungry mouths we feed, if we're doing it only to feel good about ourselves. Christian life is all about becoming more and more like Christ. It's all about how much our minds and hearts resemble His (Romans 8:29). As you submit to God during this cancer, don't be surprised if He starts a renovation project in your heart. Somewhere in the process, you'll discover your true self . . . the person God created you to be. You'll start becoming a reflection of Him. You'll radiate His light wherever you go. His love will start flowing through you to other people who are suffering. You'll feel their pain. You'll understand their fears. You'll know what to say and how to help. You'll be like Jesus. And people will want to bask in your glow. ❦

BEAUTY FOR ASHES

THE SPIRIT OF THE SOVEREIGN LORD IS
UPON ME, BECAUSE THE LORD HAS
APPOINTED ME TO BRING GOOD NEWS TO
THE POOR. HE HAS SENT ME TO COMFORT
THE BROKENHEARTED AND TO ANNOUNCE
THAT CAPTIVES WILL BE RELEASED AND
PRISONERS WILL BE FREED. HE HAS SENT ME
TO TELL THOSE WHO MOURN THAT THE
TIME OF THE LORD'S FAVOR HAS COME, AND
WITH IT, THE DAY OF GOD'S ANGER AGAINST
THEIR ENEMIES. TO ALL WHO MOURN IN
ISRAEL, HE WILL GIVE BEAUTY FOR ASHES,
JOY INSTEAD OF MOURNING, PRAISE INSTEAD
OF DESPAIR. FOR THE LORD HAS PLANTED
THEM LIKE STRONG AND GRACEFUL OAKS
FOR HIS OWN GLORY. . . . INSTEAD OF SHAME
AND DISHONOR, YOU WILL INHERIT A
DOUBLE PORTION OF PROSPERITY AND
EVERLASTING JOY.

Isaiah 61:1–3, 7

Cancer Center. The sign on the double doors was the first thing I saw every time the elevator door opened to the fourth floor. This time, instead of going straight ahead into the center, I turned left and proceeded down the hall. All the times I had been to the Cancer Center through the diagnosis and staging of my cancer, I prayed I would never have to turn left off the elevator. The sign at the end of that hall read Hematology and Oncology. I checked in at the desk and settled in for a long wait to see the oncologist. Chairs, mostly occupied, lined the walls and filled the center of the waiting room. The people were of all ages, from young children to the elderly. Some covered their bald heads with stocking caps or baseball caps. Others just left their baldness exposed. Some used canes or walkers and others were attached to IV stands. *Oh God, I don't want to be one of these people.* But deep in their eyes, I could see something we all shared . . . a desperate longing for hope.

In Isaiah 61, the prophet describes God's promise of hope for the Israelites while they would be held captive in Babylon. But He was also foretelling the coming of Jesus Christ, God's New Covenant with His people. Jesus himself read this Scripture at the synagogue in Nazareth, His boyhood home. He proclaimed himself to be the one who would bring this Good News to pass (Luke 4:18–21). Jesus himself became the ultimate sacrifice for our sin. The Lamb of God was slain on a cross instead of an unblemished lamb slain on an altar. His death redeemed us and made us acceptable in God's eyes (Romans 3:21–24). He poured out His blood to forgive our sins, and all who believe in Him can come into God's presence (Matthew 26:28). All who believe can have hope.

The Israelites put their hope in false gods and military alliances with pagan nations. They turned their hearts away from the Lord and lived in a barren hopeless wilderness (Jeremiah 17:5–6). But those who trust the Lord will be set free. He will comfort their broken hearts. They are like well-watered trees on a riverbank and will receive strength in times of crisis. They will not be bothered by heat or worry about long months of drought (Jeremiah 17:7–8). It's true, the drought of your cancer may last for several months. But through it all, you can go right on producing delicious fruit. You can have hope and receive a double portion of blessing! So trade your mourning for joy. Trade your despair for praise. Trade your ashes for beauty. Trade it all for Jesus. ❦

HEALING COME QUICKLY

> I WANT YOU TO SHARE YOUR FOOD WITH
> THE HUNGRY AND TO WELCOME POOR
> WANDERERS INTO YOUR HOMES. GIVE
> CLOTHES TO THOSE WHO NEED THEM, AND
> DO NOT HIDE FROM RELATIVES WHO NEED
> YOUR HELP. IF YOU DO THESE THINGS, YOUR
> SALVATION WILL COME LIKE THE DAWN. YES,
> YOUR HEALING WILL COME QUICKLY. YOUR
> GODLINESS WILL LEAD YOU FORWARD, AND
> THE GLORY OF THE LORD WILL PROTECT
> YOU FROM BEHIND.
>
> *Isaiah 58:7–8*

There should be a warning sign posted in our homes and on our cars, boats, and other toys: *Beware! Comfortable lifestyle may cause heart to harden.* It happens so slowly. When things are going so well in our lives, we are lulled into a false sense of security. Maybe we start to view our blessings as more of an entitlement than a gift from the Creator. I know I was much more interested in what God could do for me than what I could do for Him. I could dash into church on Sundays and get my own spiritual tank filled, but I didn't have much time to fill anyone else's. So when cancer came, I didn't expect a raft of people to come to my aid. I was amazed when people of faith showed such deep compassion for me. Their faith and actions went beyond their own personal growth and getting their own needs met. Many were cancer survivors. God had softened their hearts, and His compassion poured out through them.

The Israelites were comfortable. God had richly blessed His chosen people. Time and time again, they fell into sin and drifted away from Him. When they repented, God always forgave them. The prophet Isaiah had the difficult task of speaking God's message to these stubborn people who once again would not listen. They were practicing all the rituals of worship correctly but showed no compassion for the oppressed (Isaiah 58:1–7). Their hearts had hardened toward God. Isaiah's words brought a message of forgiveness and hope as he foretold of God's future blessing. God's promise through Isaiah is the same for us today. With the risen Christ in our heart, our light will shine out from the darkness. The Lord will guide us continually, watering our life when we are dry and keeping us healthy like a well-watered garden (Isaiah 58:10–11). Our life reflects His. We become His hands and feet. We bring kindness, charity, and generosity with us wherever we go.

So we shouldn't get too comfortable. God knows the difference between the obedient followers and pretenders. He expects more than dutiful worship and religious doctrine. Our faith is not about "what's in it for me." It's all about Him. And the real evidence is in how we treat people. That doesn't mean you should rush out and fill your calendar tomorrow with volunteer work at the local soup kitchen. We are not healed on our own power. God alone heals our sin and cures our disease (Jeremiah 30:17). But when you submit to Him and let Christ reign in your life, your heart slowly softens. The kindness and compassion of Jesus naturally start to overflow to those around you. Your light will spring forth like the dawn and your healing will come quickly. Your godly behavior will lead you forward and prepare the way for His deeper work inside you (Psalm 85:13). His glory will protect you from behind. What an awesome way to live. ❧

PITY PARTY

LORD, DON'T HOLD BACK YOUR TENDER
MERCIES FROM ME. MY ONLY HOPE IS IN
YOUR UNFAILING LOVE AND FAITHFULNESS.
Psalm 40:11

*N*othing changed. My husband traveled a lot for business. He traveled right through chemo class and much of my chemo. My son was a senior in college and my daughter was a senior in high school. My cancer didn't alter their busy schedules one bit. There were still groceries to buy, messes to clean up, laundry to do, and meals to cook. Mom still did all the things moms do. Most of the time, I liked being treated as though nothing had changed. It helped me feel normal and I needed to feel normal. But sometimes I wanted to scream. *Do I have to do everything around this house? Would it be too much to ask you to hang up your coat or unload the dishwasher? Don't you people realize I have cancer? People die from this, you know!* Throw in the numb fingers and toes, sore joints, bald head, and missing eyebrows, and I could have myself one big pity party.

It's easy to focus on our complaints. It's so easy to quickly forget about God's mercies. When I fall into a pit of despair, King David reminds me of all the good things God does for me:

* He forgives all my sins
* He heals my diseases
* He ransoms me from death and destruction
* He surrounds me with loving-kindness and compassion
* He satisfies my desires so that my youth is renewed like the eagle's

�֍ He gives righteousness and justice for me when I am treated unfairly (Psalm 103:1–6).

Our God is amazing. He pours all of these blessings on us, and we don't deserve a single one. I forget sometimes. I whine and complain about my circumstances. I might even feel a little sorry for myself. Sometimes I try to control and manipulate people and situations that don't meet my expectations. But God's steadfast love and tender mercy is greater than any sin. And best of all, His mercies start fresh every day to keep me from complete destruction. His unfailing love never ends (Lamentations 3:22–24).

God's faithfulness is perfect and His love is absolute. The next time this cancer gets you down and you decide to throw yourself a pity party, take a look at David's list. Better yet, read it every day until it becomes permanently etched on your heart. All the good things in your life, everything good and perfect, come directly from your Father in heaven (James 1:17). All His blessings, all His tender mercies, and all His compassion are yours in Jesus Christ. Praise God and call off the party! ✺

His Plan, Not Mine

> Look here, you people who say, "Today
> or tomorrow we are going to a
> certain town and will stay there a
> year. We will do business there and
> make a profit." How do you know
> what will happen tomorrow? For
> your life is like the morning fog—it's
> here a little while, then it's gone.
> What you ought to say is, "If the Lord
> wants us to, we will live and do
> this or that."
>
> *James 4:13–15*

I don't have a five- or ten-year plan anymore. I don't even have a master plan for my retirement. It's not that I don't think I'll be around. I have big plans to be around. My problem is, I've always had big plans! Sometimes I got so busy planning the "next thing," I missed out on the present. Today's activities simply became checks on my to-do list. Life was a little like climbing a mountain. I could become so focused on reaching the top that I missed all the beautiful scenery along the way. Sometimes I missed out on the spontaneous side trips God had planned to delight me and teach me more about His character. *God, you can't possibly expect me to deviate from "the plan." It might throw me off schedule.*

Breast cancer shuffled my plans and my priorities. I've learned that life on this earth is short no matter how many years I live. James reminds me to have an eternal perspective on my life plans. My plans will always fall short of my expectations if I leave God out. My past, present, and future are all in His hands, so it's pointless to plan without Him. I have learned more than once how easily He can step in at any time and rearrange things. I'm learning to plan ahead but to always keep God in the center. By listening to the still, small voice in my spirit, I'm more willing to deviate from the plan when God has a better idea. I am learning that His plans are always bigger and more astounding than any plan I could ever dream up on my own (Isaiah 55:8–9). When I live for God every day and am obedient to His daily guidance, it shouldn't matter when my life ends. I know I will have fulfilled His plan for me. *His* plan, not mine.

Breast cancer will probably change your plans too. It might cause you to take a closer look at your priorities. When your Father looks down from heaven, even your grandest grown-up plans are like toddler plans to Him. He has so much more in store for you. When your treatment is over and the worst has passed, you can easily fall back into your old schedule. Or you can make Him the center of all your plans and start storing treasures in heaven where cancer can never reach (Matthew 6:20). How? Start every day with a grateful heart. Know that every single day you wake up breathing is a blessing from God. Then open your Bible and ask Him to show you what exciting thing He has planned for you today. When you hear His still, small voice, be obedient to His guidance. Now, how's that for a plan? ❦

A Son's Faith

> FUTURE GENERATIONS WILL ALSO SERVE
> HIM. OUR CHILDREN WILL HEAR ABOUT THE
> WONDERS OF THE LORD. HIS RIGHTEOUS
> ACTS WILL BE TOLD TO THOSE YET UNBORN.
> THEY WILL HEAR ABOUT EVERYTHING
> HE HAS DONE.
> *Psalm 22:30–31*

When my cancer was suspected, I went straight to the prayer chapel in my local church with my family in tow. It was the first of many visits where prayer ministers and elders laid hands on me and anointed my head with oil (James 5:14–15). My son was a senior in college at the time. I didn't know if he came for some serious prayer or if he was just there to support his mom. I suspect the latter. He didn't say much during the whole cancer ordeal except, "Mom, I know you can beat this. You're the strongest person I know." He took the whole thing in stride, but I suspected he was afraid. What kid wouldn't be? I didn't learn until much later about the strength of his faith. One of his friends shared with me that my son always spoke with strong conviction about God's will to heal me. His faith made a significant impact on his friends.

How we cope in times of crisis can be a huge witness for our children. When cancer struck, I'd like to think my son's faith increased by watching his mother turn first to the Lord. I'd like to think it wasn't the first time he watched me lean on God in times of trial. We teach our children to choose the right path, to walk in faith and not fear, so they will stay the course when they grow up (Proverbs 22:6). They learn by example how to meet a crisis head on. They learn to overcome, not run. If we let our children witness His power and mighty miracles in our lives, they will tell the next generation about the glorious deeds of the Lord (Psalm 78:4). God promises our families will flourish for as long as the sky remains above the earth if we teach His Word to our children (Deuteronomy 11:19–21).

If you're like me, there is only one thing that hurts you more than your cancer, and that's how your children have to cope with it. Right now, they may be paralyzed with fear. They talk to people and hear the news just like you do. They field daily questions and comments about their mother's cancer. Pray that through your witness, your calm spirit, and your healing, your children see the Lord's glory at work in your cancer (Psalm 90:15–16). Pray that the Lord would hold your children in His tender arms and minister faith and contentment into their hearts. Pray for the peace of Christ that surpasses all human understanding to guard their hearts and minds against fear and anxiety (Philippians 4:7). It's hard to imagine, but God loves them even more than you do. He promised that His salvation extends to the children's children of those who are faithful to His covenant (Psalm 103:17–18). Let your children hear about the wonders of the Lord! Their faith might someday amaze you. 🐦

A FARMER WENT OUT TO PLANT SOME SEED.
AS HE SCATTERED IT ACROSS HIS FIELD,
SOME SEED FELL ON A FOOTPATH, WHERE IT
WAS STEPPED ON, AND THE BIRDS CAME AND
ATE IT. OTHER SEED FELL ON SHALLOW SOIL
WITH UNDERLYING ROCK. THIS SEED BEGAN
TO GROW, BUT SOON IT WITHERED AND
DIED FOR LACK OF MOISTURE. OTHER SEED
FELL AMONG THORNS THAT SHOT UP AND
CHOKED OUT THE TENDER BLADES. STILL
OTHER SEED FELL ON FERTILE SOIL. THIS
SEED GREW AND PRODUCED A CROP ONE
HUNDRED TIMES AS MUCH AS HAD
BEEN PLANTED.

Luke 8:5–8

ey Mom! I stole the shampoo and conditioner out of your shower. I kinda figured you wouldn't need it. What a relief to hear her joke about my bald head. My daughter was an active high school senior at the time of my diagnosis and treatment. She was an on-fire Christian and heavily involved in youth ministry at church. From a coping perspective, I thought we were home free. She was a pillar of faith during the whole cancer ordeal. That is, until I lost my hair. Thank God she was out of town at a dance team competition when my husband shaved it off. She would hardly look at me when I picked her up at the airport sporting my new wig. When we got home, she went immediately to her room, closed the door, and sobbed into her pillow like a little girl. *I won't look at you! I can't!* Reality came crashing down. Her mom had cancer. She really did have cancer.

Her heart was broken. And so was mine. I prayed that the young tender roots of her faith reached down deep enough to weather this storm. Jesus taught that the seeds of faith could be planted in four types of soil. The hard path represents those who hear the message but refuse to believe. The rocky soil people have young shallow roots and believe for a while, but wilt when the hot winds of testing blow. The thorny ground people let the pleasures of the world choke out God's promises. But the seeds planted in fertile soil represent those who cling to God's Word and reap a huge harvest (Luke 8:12–15).

The hot winds of testing could have wilted my daughter, or she could have turned to her busy high school schedule to escape reality. But she chose to cling to God. My cancer took her through the valley of weeping where the roots of her faith grew deeper. Surrounded by love and good Christian leaders, the winds of testing drove her into God's arms where she experienced His faithfulness (Psalm 84:5–7). He took her mourning and turned it into joyful dancing (Psalm 30:11). Literally. A few months later, I joined her in a parents' dance routine in front of a gym full of people. In spite of our giggling and with a little help from God, my wig even stayed on my head.

As the hot winds of cancer swirl around you, you can take heart in knowing the Lord's hand of protection is on you and your household. He has fortified the bars of your gates and blessed your children within (Psalm 147:13). Your children may shed tears over your cancer, but God can turn your cancer and their tears into a mighty fertilizer that drives their little roots deeper into the soil of His love (Psalm 126:4–6). He can turn their mourning into joyful dancing! And you'll be dancing with them. ❦

A Husband's Strength

> David shouted in reply, "You come to
> me with sword, spear, and javelin, but I
> come to you in the name of the Lord
> Almighty—the God of the armies of
> Israel, whom you have defied."
> *1 Samuel 17:45*

The doctor called with the biopsy report, and for two days, my husband never said a word. I started to worry. What was he thinking? What was he feeling? Finally he spoke. He was embarrassed to tell me he had been worried about himself. Who would drink coffee and read the paper with him every morning if I were gone? Who would retire with him? With that conversation out of the way, he put on his manager hat. He was determined to treat this cancer like any other event in life. It was business as usual. My husband . . . always the pillar of strength in times of trouble . . . always the eternal optimist.

Now, David was an optimist. With God on his side, he always knew there was a way out of every trap the enemy set for him. He knew no problem or no circumstance was too difficult for the Creator of the heavens and earth (Psalm 124:7–8). As a shepherd boy, he defeated Goliath with a stone and a sling because he knew his strength came from God and the Lord does not need weapons to rescue His people (1 Samuel 17:45–51). David went on to become a great warrior and Israel's greatest king. He experienced glorious victories in his lifetime because his faith in God never wavered.

My husband probably didn't know it at the time, but his optimism—his underlying faith—was a spiritual gift from God. He didn't understand until two years later when he waged his own battle with unemployment just how badly he needed Christ. This time it was his event, not mine. Through it, he learned that Christ alone was the source of all his strength. He could do all things through Him and nothing without Him (Philippians 4:13). God's wonderful plan wove our experiences together and yoked us spiritually so we could walk in faith together. With Christ at the center, our shared faith forms a triple-braided cord that can conquer adversity with a supernatural strength and power that neither of us could manage on our own (Ecclesiastes 4:12).

If you are sharing your cancer experience with a spouse, you might be surprised by his reaction. He may withdraw to cope with his own feelings, or he may take over and attempt to cope with yours. He may do anything in between. Whatever his reaction might be, trust that the Lord can use him to comfort and strengthen you. God can use this adversity to knit you closer together. He can even use your cancer to draw your spouse to Him (1 Corinthians 7:16). Your cancer might come at you with sword, spear, and javelin, but together, you can stand against it in the name of the Lord Almighty. For He is the source of all your strength. ❦

Hunger Pains

YOU MUST CRAVE PURE SPIRITUAL MILK SO
THAT YOU CAN GROW INTO THE FULLNESS
OF YOUR SALVATION. CRY OUT FOR THIS
NOURISHMENT AS A BABY CRIES FOR MILK,
NOW THAT YOU HAVE HAD A TASTE OF
THE LORD'S KINDNESS.

1 Peter 2:2–3

I remember bringing my son home from the hospital. As a first-time mom, I knew nothing about babies except what I read in books and learned in the newborn class at the hospital. How hard could it be for a smart college graduate like me? I would just feed him, change him, put him to sleep, and watch him grow. Right? Not quite. As much as I thought I knew, I wasn't prepared for the next few weeks. He nursed every two hours, around the clock. Just when I drifted off to sleep, he woke up crying and hungry. I feared I would never sleep again and this ravenous child would become a permanent attachment.

Crying for milk was a natural instinct for my newborn son. Healthy babies need nourishment to grow and develop, just as spiritual babies need to feed on the knowledge of God. I was a baby Christian before my diagnosis. I was usually more concerned with what I wanted to do than what God might have in mind. All that changed when I tasted the Lord's kindness during my cancer. When He reached down into my life and comforted me, His love became real. When every detail of my treatment fell perfectly into place, my knowledge of Him became personal. I had a deep hunger to learn more. I was like a spiritual newborn with a ravenous spiritual appetite. As I sought to know Him better through Bible study and prayer, I gradually became more in tune with God's desires for me. Just as my son thrived on mother's milk, the pure spiritual milk found in Christ began to nourish my character. I found myself growing in patience, faith, obedience, and my capacity to love others (2 Peter 1:5–9).

It doesn't matter where you are in your cancer journey. It doesn't matter how spiritually mature you were when cancer struck. Once you taste the Lord's kindness at the core of your suffering, you'll cry out for more of Him as a baby cries for milk. He won't mind if your hunger pains come every two hours or every two minutes. He never sleeps (Psalm 121:4). Seek Christ with all your heart. Learn all you can about Him. The more you know, the more like Him you'll become (Ephesians 1:16–17). Drink in His pure spiritual milk and let it nourish your spirit. Like a proud parent, the Lord will watch you grow into the child He created you to be. ❦

Do Over

> THEN THE LORD SPOKE TO JONAH A SECOND
> TIME: "GET UP AND GO TO THE GREAT CITY
> OF NINEVEH, AND DELIVER THE MESSAGE OF
> JUDGMENT I HAVE GIVEN YOU." THIS TIME
> JONAH OBEYED THE LORD'S COMMAND AND
> WENT TO NINEVEH, A CITY SO LARGE THAT
> IT TOOK THREE DAYS TO SEE IT ALL.
>
> *Jonah 3:1–3*

*R*emember playing games as a kid and our playmates would give us a "do over"? Well, God gave Jonah a do over. He told him to go to the Assyrian capital city of Nineveh and warn the people of the Lord's judgment against them. The Assyrians were Israel's greatest enemy and Jonah hated them. So instead, he boarded a ship heading in the opposite direction in an attempt to escape from God. But God caused a violent storm and Jonah was thrown into the sea where he was swallowed by a great fish (Jonah 1). After three days and three nights inside the fish, God heard Jonah's prayer and rescued him. He gave Jonah a second chance to participate in His work. This time, Jonah obeyed. He preached God's message in the streets of Nineveh. As a result, the people repented and were delivered from God's judgment (Jonah 3:5–10).

I remember a time when I disobeyed God. Several years ago a friend and co-worker passed away from ovarian cancer. Many times in the last few months of her suffering, I had a strong prompting in my spirit to go see her. *But I don't want to go to Nineveh!* And I didn't. I suspect breast cancer is a little like being in the belly of a fish. I don't know if God sent me there. I do know

He sent me back to Nineveh. This time, I obeyed. And God expanded the assignment. Today I lead a cancer care ministry. I counsel, mentor, and pray with people suffering from all types of cancer. The people I touch are blessed. And so am I. All because God, in His mercy, gave me a do over . . . a second chance to participate in the work of His kingdom . . . a second chance to be His hands and feet.

Has God ever sent you to Nineveh? As He did with Jonah, He may prompt you to do things you don't want to do. He may want you to testify through your cancer to His awesome power and faithfulness. He may want you to care for the sick or serve Him in a way that's way out of your comfort zone. And you might want to turn and run away. But you can't escape His presence, no matter where you run (Psalm 139:7–12). And you can't seek Him and run from Him at the same time. Don't worry if you've already jumped on a ship going in the opposite direction and feel unworthy of serving Him. God is patient and forgiving. He loves you even when you disappoint Him. Turn to Him. In His mercy, He'll give you a do over. Maybe I'll see you in Nineveh. *

PUT ON YOUR ARMOR

> PUT ON ALL OF GOD'S ARMOR SO THAT YOU
> WILL BE ABLE TO STAND FIRM AGAINST ALL
> STRATEGIES AND TRICKS OF THE DEVIL. FOR
> WE ARE NOT FIGHTING AGAINST PEOPLE
> MADE OF FLESH AND BLOOD, BUT AGAINST
> THE EVIL RULERS AND AUTHORITIES OF THE
> UNSEEN WORLD, AGAINST THOSE MIGHTY
> POWERS OF DARKNESS WHO RULE THIS
> WORLD, AND AGAINST WICKED SPIRITS IN
> THE HEAVENLY REALMS. USE EVERY PIECE OF
> GOD'S ARMOR TO RESIST THE ENEMY IN THE
> TIME OF EVIL, SO THAT AFTER THE BATTLE
> YOU WILL STILL BE STANDING FIRM.
>
> *Ephesians 6:11–13*

I don't like to think about spiritual warfare. It brings up thoughts of scary little demons hiding under every rock and behind every corner just waiting to launch an attack. Coming out of the breast cancer battle, the thought of fighting more "evil rulers and authorities of the unseen world," "mighty powers of darkness," and "wicked spirits in the heavenly realms" is a bit unsettling. But the Bible makes it clear there is a powerful enemy who wants to defeat Christ's church. We become the Enemy's adversary too when we align ourselves with Christ. Now that's scary. But here's the good news. Christ already defeated the Enemy at Calvary. Oh, the Enemy will keep trying to convince us otherwise. He'll keep lying and conniving to keep us from believing so we won't walk in the victory Christ won for us. But our job is not to keep fighting him. Our job is to resist him daily with the truth of his defeat. When we resist, he flees (James 4:7). And God gave us an arsenal of weapons to do it.

God's weapons break down every lie the Enemy uses to keep us from knowing Christ (2 Corinthians 10:3–6). He has given us the Holy Spirit and full body armor to resist the Enemy's attack and stand true to God. With the belt of truth we can discern the Enemy's lies. The body armor of righteousness protects our hearts and ensures God's love for us. The shoes of peace give us courage and motivation to go out and proclaim the Good News of Christ. The shield of faith protects us from insults, setbacks, and other fiery arrows the Enemy launches against us. It keeps our eyes focused on Christ instead of our circumstances. The helmet protects our minds from doubting God's promise of salvation. The sword is the Word of God (Ephesians 6:14–17). Anytime the Enemy tempts us with a lie, we just grab our Bibles and counter with Scripture that refutes it . . . just as Christ resisted Satan in the wilderness (Matthew 4:1–11). Once you realize the Bible is your most powerful weapon against the Enemy it will never gather dust on a shelf again.

You don't have to worry about demons hiding behind every corner, planning and scheming to steal your healing. Jesus gave you authority over them so you have nothing to fear (Luke 10:19). You have prayer, faith, hope, love, and the Word of God on your side. The Holy Spirit within you is far greater than all the powers of darkness combined (1 John 4:4). Besides, God has already disarmed the evil rulers and authorities through His victory on the cross (Colossians 2:15). So put on your armor! The enemy can make empty threats all day long, and you'll just yawn, shrug your shoulders, and say, "Oh, it's just you." 🌿

EXPECT A MIRACLE

THINK OF IT—THE LORD HAS HEALED ME! I
WILL SING HIS PRAISES WITH INSTRUMENTS
EVERY DAY OF MY LIFE IN THE TEMPLE
OF THE LORD.

Isaiah 38:20

Hezekiah was one of Judah's most faithful kings. When he became deathly ill, the prophet Isaiah told him to set his affairs in order, for he would not recover from this illness. Hezekiah wept bitterly and prayed fervently to the Lord. He grieved that his life would be cut short and he would never again see his friends or laugh with those who live in this world. He pleaded and pleaded to the Lord, delirious with anguish, until his eyes grew tired of looking to heaven for help. God heard Hezekiah's prayer. He saw his tears and healed him. Hezekiah understood that God spared his life and his desperate prayer had brought healing and forgiveness. He praised God for the good that came out of his suffering. He vowed to sing praises to God every day for the rest of his life (Isaiah 38:1–20).

I wish every day was a Hezekiah day. On those days, I stand humbled in front of the mirror. I look in amazement at my thick hair and my body restored to health. Think of it! The Lord has healed me! I drop to my knees and the words of the psalmists echo deep in my heart. "Because he bends down and listens, I will pray as long as I have breath! Death had its hands around my throat; the terrors of the grave overtook me. I saw only trouble and sorrow. Then I called on the name of the Lord: 'Please, Lord, save me!' . . . I was facing death, and then he saved me" (Psalm 116:2–4, 6). "I will praise you, my God and King, and bless your name forever and ever" (Psalm 145:1). "I will sing praises to my God even with my dying breath" (Psalm 146:2). "I will honor you as long as I live, lifting up my hands to you in prayer. . . . I will praise you with songs of joy" (Psalm 63:4–5). I can't sing praises and worship the Lord without my arms lifted up to the heavens. Because He heard my prayer . . . He saw my tears . . . and He healed me. He changed my life forever.

Sincere faith and fervent prayer can change your situation, no matter how desperate. I've seen it happen many times. Someone will come into the prayer chapel in a serious health crisis. Family, friends, and prayer ministers pray fervently for as long as the Holy Spirit guides and directs. Prayers will continue for days, through every test, every doctor visit, and every surgery. And then one day, a loved one calls with a praise report. *The doctor was amazed! The cancer is gone!* God's Word is the final authority. Plead and plead your case to the Lord until your eyes grow tired of looking to heaven for help. Expect a miracle. Expect a Hezekiah day. ❦

PRODUCE MUCH FRUIT

> YES, I AM THE VINE; YOU ARE THE
> BRANCHES. THOSE WHO REMAIN IN ME, AND
> I IN THEM, WILL PRODUCE MUCH FRUIT.
> FOR APART FROM ME YOU CAN DO
> NOTHING. ANYONE WHO PARTS FROM ME IS
> THROWN AWAY LIKE A USELESS BRANCH AND
> WITHERS. SUCH BRANCHES ARE GATHERED
> INTO A PILE TO BE BURNED. BUT IF YOU
> STAY JOINED TO ME AND MY WORDS REMAIN
> IN YOU, YOU MAY ASK ANY REQUEST YOU
> LIKE, AND IT WILL BE GRANTED! MY TRUE
> DISCIPLES PRODUCE MUCH FRUIT. THIS
> BRINGS GREAT GLORY TO MY FATHER.
>
> *John 15:5–8*

I love to garden. Every spring I trim away the weak and dead branches from my plants and shrubbery. The remaining branches grow new shoots, the foliage thickens, and the plants grow healthier. The pruned branches decay in the compost pile. It's a lot like my relationship with Christ. He is the vine and I'm a branch. If I stay in fellowship with Him as a branch stays connected to a vine in my garden, I remain vital, healthy, and produce fruit (Galatians 5:22–23). I bask in the Father's love, my prayers are answered, and my joy overflows (John 15:9–11). But if I get separated from Christ, I can do nothing. I'll likely wither away and be tossed into a compost pile somewhere with all the other useless branches.

It was clear to me. There were no advantages to living apart from Christ. Living in fellowship with Him would be my ultimate goal in life. Paul said everything else is worthless in comparison (Philippians 3:7–8). Cancer gave me a taste of what living in God's presence is all about. It made me long for Jesus twenty-four hours a day, seven days a week. I wanted to live in Him as He lives in me, and have health, peace, and abundant joy forever. But as life gradually returned to normal, I learned it takes discipline. The world continually tries to distract me from spending time with God. I might make a point to get up early and spend time in the Bible, and the phone rings or my e-mails take over. I might set aside time for Bible study and prayer over lunch, and I lose track of time and work straight through. I might plan to catch up with God later in the evening, after my meeting at church. Even work for the kingdom can keep me from spending personal time with the Savior. I get home, I crawl into bed determined to pray, and I can't stay awake. The day is over. Without even realizing it, I've cut myself off from my Life Source. And without spiritual nourishment I can't produce much fruit. If I'm not careful, I can end up like those straggly branches I trim off my shrubbery.

What a comfort to know God lives in all who believe (1 John 4:15)! He lives in all who obey His teachings, remain faithful, and love others the same way He loves us (1 John 2:24; 3:24; John 15:12). And He shows up, even when we miss our appointments with Him. You have been clothed with a brand-new nature that is continually renewed as you learn more and more about Christ (Colossians 3:10). So let heaven fill your thoughts (Colossians 3:2). Take creative steps to "remain in Christ." Put the Bible on your nightstand and open it before your feet hit the floor every morning. Listen to Bible tapes or CDs on your way to work or during your daily workout. Do whatever it takes to stay vital and healthy and connected to the Lord in prayer. Bring glory to your Father. Produce much fruit. ❧

The Best Is Yet To Come

> THAT IS WHAT THE SCRIPTURES MEAN WHEN
> THEY SAY, "NO EYE HAS SEEN, NO EAR HAS
> HEARD, AND NO MIND HAS IMAGINED WHAT
> GOD HAS PREPARED FOR THOSE WHO
> LOVE HIM."
> *1 Corinthians 2:9*

It was a year of celebration . . . a year of counting our blessings. Chemo was over but the Minnesota winter wasn't. My husband surprised me with a trip to St. Thomas in the Virgin Islands. He rented a private villa nestled in the hills on the northern side of the island. I stood on the deck overlooking the beautiful tropical gardens below and the rocky coastline a short distance away wondering how anything could be more perfect. We spent the afternoons building sand castles on Megan's Bay. It didn't even matter that no hair grew under my straw beach hat. Wading in the crystal-clear water watching the sailboats drifting in the ocean breeze, I marveled at the beauty of His creation and my presence in the midst of it. The Lord healed me! I have a heavenly Father who loves and cares for me. Later that summer, after I had regained some strength, we went mountain hiking at Lake O'Hara in the Canadian Rockies. Again, I was awestruck by God's creation as I hiked up the mountain trails and drank in the beauty of the blue lakes and valleys below and snow-covered peaks against the clear sky above. Could I be more blessed?

Yes! In Isaiah 65:17 the Lord said: "Look! I am creating new heavens and a new earth so wonderful that *no one will even think about the old one anymore*" (emphasis added). I can't imagine. A new heaven and earth so wonderful that I could *forget* the miles of white sand beach and clear blue waters of a sun-soaked Caribbean paradise . . . so wonderful I could *forget* the beauty of snow-capped mountains reaching into the clouds . . . so wonderful all my blessings today will seem insignificant. I can't imagine how the Lord could top this life with the one yet to come!

I know. We have troubles in this world (John 16:33). I watch the news and read the newspaper just as you do. We all suffer personal tragedy and hardship. Some of us suffer from breast cancer. But God sent the Holy Spirit to comfort and guide us. The Holy Spirit gives us hope and courage to endure suffering and to press on in this life. We don't have to look at the troubles we can see right now. We can look forward to what we have not yet seen. Our troubles today will soon be over, but the joys to come will last forever (2 Corinthians 4:18).

No matter how much you are suffering, one thing never changes. Your future belongs to God. God provides the hope in things that you cannot see, both in this life and the next. No eye has seen, no ear has heard, and no mind has imagined the future God has prepared for you. Let go of the cares and concerns of this world and look forward to what you have not yet seen. It promises to be so wonderful you'll never look back. And nothing in all the earth can ever take away what God has promised. The best is yet to come! ❧

AND THERE WAS A WOMAN IN THE CROWD
WHO HAD HAD A HEMORRHAGE FOR TWELVE
YEARS. SHE HAD SUFFERED A GREAT DEAL
FROM MANY DOCTORS THROUGH THE
YEARS AND HAD SPENT EVERYTHING SHE
HAD TO PAY THEM, BUT SHE HAD GOTTEN
NO BETTER. IN FACT, SHE WAS WORSE. SHE
HAD HEARD ABOUT JESUS, SO SHE CAME UP
BEHIND HIM THROUGH THE CROWD AND
TOUCHED THE FRINGE OF HIS ROBE. FOR
SHE THOUGHT TO HERSELF, "IF I CAN JUST
TOUCH HIS CLOTHING, I WILL BE HEALED."
IMMEDIATELY THE BLEEDING STOPPED,
AND SHE COULD FEEL THAT SHE
HAD BEEN HEALED!

Mark 5:25–29

Several years ago a friend was diagnosed with an aggressive type of cancer. It was before my own cancer journey, but I could see how badly she needed the Lord. When I suggested prayer and gave her a couple of books on faith and healing, her response broke my heart. *All that religion didn't work for me when I was well. Why should it work for me now that I'm sick?* She was disillusioned by her experience growing up in the church. Somewhere along the line she had been deeply disappointed. The actions of people who claimed to be Christians didn't match the teachings of the church. Her disappointment kept her from seeking God.

The hemorrhaging woman in the Scripture took an entirely different approach. For twelve years she suffered, most likely from some kind of menstrual or uterine disorder. She spent everything she had on doctors, and her condition only worsened. By Jewish law, her bleeding would have made her ritually unclean and excluded her from most social contact. She wanted so desperately to be healed, but she knew if she touched Jesus her bleeding would cause Him to be unclean. So she found another way. She fought her way through the crowd just to touch the fringe of His robe. She didn't let her circumstances and past disappointments keep her from seeking God. Jesus honored her faith and healed her instantly. *Daughter, your faith has made you well* (Mark 5:34).

If the best breast cancer doctor in the world lived in your town, you wouldn't hesitate to seek her counsel. I hope you would be her patient. But daughter, the best breast cancer doctor in all creation lives right in your heart! He is the Lord who heals all your diseases (Exodus 15:26; Psalm 103:3). Regardless of past experiences or disappointments, you can always approach your heavenly Father. My friend's disillusionment kept her from turning to Him, even when her medical prognosis looked hopeless. But the bleeding woman let nothing stop her from seeking Jesus. Let nothing stop you. 🌿

And Then Some

> As they approached the Temple, a man
> lame from birth was being carried in.
> Each day he was put beside the Temple
> gate, the one called the Beautiful
> Gate, so he could beg from the people
> going into the Temple. When he saw
> Peter and John about to enter, he
> asked them for some money. Peter and
> John looked at him intently, and Peter
> said, "Look at us!" The lame man
> looked at them eagerly, expecting a
> gift. But Peter said, "I don't have any
> money for you. But I'll give you what
> I have. In the name of Jesus Christ of
> Nazareth, get up and walk!"
>
> *Acts 3:2–6*

Imagine what would happen if we gave our children control of our family decisions. We would play all day, buy anything we wanted, eat Popsicles for dinner, and make regular trips to Disney World. Left to their own resources, young children simply don't have the wisdom and maturity to know what to ask for or do what's best for them. I wonder if my heavenly Father thinks the same thing when He hears my toddler-sized thoughts and prayers. He wants to give me *infinitely* more than I could ever ask for or hope (Ephesians 3:20). His thoughts are God-sized (Isaiah 55:9). When I prayed for healing, the Lord healed me and gave me a cancer ministry. When I was lonely and longed for friendship, He surrounded me with amazing Christian brothers and sisters and more fun and fellowship than I could ever dream of. When I wrote a few devotions to comfort a friend, the Lord turned it into a book. I ask Him to solve a small problem, and He always has something better in mind!

Now the crippled beggar had a problem. Each day he was placed beside the temple gate so he could beg for money from the people going to the temple. He asked Peter and John for money, but the Lord gave him something better. He restored the use of his legs. No wonder he jumped, leaped, and praised God (Acts 3:8)! God gave him exactly what he needed to solve the bigger problem. With his crippled legs healed, he would never have to beg for money again.

What's your biggest problem today? Perhaps you're troubled by a child's behavior or a friend's indifference. Maybe it's something bigger, like a bad pathology report or serious side effects from your chemo. Don't be surprised if God gives you a God-sized answer to a toddler-sized prayer. He wants to give you a whole new life and help for *all* your problems, even those you may not know about. Just as you know what's best for your children, your heavenly Father always knows what's best for you. You might not get exactly what you want, but you'll always get exactly what you need . . . and then some. ❦

A Far Greater Power

"Be strong and courageous! Don't be
afraid of the king of Assyria or his
mighty army, for there is a power far
greater on our side! He may have a
great army, but they are just men. We
have the Lord our God to help us and
to fight our battles for us!" These
words greatly encouraged the people.

2 Chronicles 32:7–8

When King Sennacherib of Assyria threatened to attack Jerusalem, King Hezekiah took two important steps. First, he did everything within his human power to protect the city. In a brilliant military strategy, he blocked the springs outside the city and channeled the water through an underground tunnel. This way, the people would have water during a long confrontation, but the enemy would have none. He strengthened his defenses by repairing the wall, adding to the fortifications, constructing a second wall outside the first, and manufacturing large numbers of weapons and shields. Then, He trusted God. He told the people they had nothing to fear. They had a power far greater than the Assyrian army on their side (2 Chronicles 32:1–5, 30).

But King Sennacherib wasn't impressed. Instead, he mocked the Lord: "Surely you must realize what I and the other kings of Assyria before me have done to all the people of the earth! Were any of the gods of those nations able to rescue their people from my power? Name just one time when any god, anywhere, was able to rescue his people from me! What makes you think your God can do any better?" (vv. 13–14). Even when King Sennacherib insulted God and Hezekiah in an attempt to terrify the people, Hezekiah didn't give in to fear. He cried out to his Father in heaven and the Lord heard his prayer. He sent an angel to destroy the Assyrian army and there was peace at last throughout the land (2 Chronicles 32:20–22).

If breast cancer could talk, it might sound a bit like King Sennacherib. *Surely you must realize what my relatives and I have done to all the people of the earth! What makes you think your God can rescue you?* Do you hear the voice of cancer mocking you and your Lord? Then follow Hezekiah's example. Take every step within your power to solve the situation. Find the best doctors you can find. Read all you can read. Be informed and make the best possible treatment decisions. And then commit the entire situation to God in prayer. Trust Him for the outcome. The Assyrian army didn't scare Hezekiah because he knew God was on his side. He knew victory against them would not come by force or strength but by His Spirit (Zechariah 4:6). So be strong and courageous! There is no need to fear any attack mounted against you. There is no need to listen to cancer's mocking voice. There is a far greater power on your side. ❧

Just Do It!

THE LORD, YOUR REDEEMER, THE HOLY
ONE OF ISRAEL, SAYS: I AM THE LORD YOUR
GOD, WHO TEACHES YOU WHAT IS GOOD
AND LEADS YOU ALONG THE PATHS YOU
SHOULD FOLLOW. OH, THAT YOU HAD
LISTENED TO MY COMMANDS! THEN YOU
WOULD HAVE HAD PEACE FLOWING LIKE A
GENTLE RIVER AND RIGHTEOUSNESS
ROLLING LIKE WAVES.
Isaiah 48:17–18

God has made His will known to us in the Scriptures. It's not a great mystery what we should and shouldn't do. I didn't rob any banks today and will not likely go out and commit adultery or murder. But cancer brought me to a whole new level of understanding obedience. When God prompts me to go next door and meet a new neighbor, He expects me to do it. When He prompts me to offer prayer for a distressed woman waiting in the oncologist's office, He expects me to do it. When He prompts me to help a needy family, He expects me to do it. When a loved one or friend makes a rude or insensitive remark, He expects me to hold my tongue. I don't know about you, but I can still come up with lots of excuses for disobedience. *I'm too busy. What will people think? I don't want to get involved. How dare he speak to me that way!*

Like any parent, God expects His children to obey everything exactly as He tells us. He's not impressed with our excuses or our human reasoning. Saul found out the consequences of disobedience. Only the priests could offer sacrifices according to Old

Testament law. But as an army of Philistines approached, he grew fearful and impatient waiting for Samuel. So he took matters into his own hands. He personally offered the pre-battle sacrifice. He lost his kingdom as a result of his disobedience (1 Samuel 13:8–14). God also gave specific instructions to the Israelites as they were traveling through the desert on the way to the Promised Land. But they wandered the desert for forty years as punishment for their countless acts of disobedience. Only their descendents and Caleb and Joshua made it to their final destination. Even Moses couldn't enter the Promised Land because he disobeyed God's instructions for providing water to the people (Numbers 20:12). Instead, God allowed him to view the Promised Land from a distance (Deuteronomy 34:1–4).

God's commands are clear. If we know what to do and don't do it, it's disobedience (James 4:17). If we let the concerns of this life distract us, it's disobedience (Matthew 8:21–22). If we make a decision or a public commitment to obey and we don't, it's disobedience (Matthew 21:28–31; Luke 6:46). If you're like me, you fall short. But God knows your heart (1 Chronicles 28:9). With a pure heart, you can come to God with bold confidence and receive whatever you request because you obey Him and do the things that please Him (1 John 3:21–22). So just do it! Don't let the opportunity to serve, pray for someone, or minister to someone in need pass you by. God will bless your obedience with peace flowing like a gentle river and righteousness rolling like waves! ✦

TOTALLY SOLD OUT

> LATER ON GOD TESTED ABRAHAM'S FAITH
> AND OBEDIENCE. "ABRAHAM!" GOD CALLED.
> "YES," HE REPLIED. "HERE I AM." "TAKE
> YOUR SON, YOUR ONLY SON—YES, ISAAC,
> WHOM YOU LOVE SO MUCH—AND GO TO
> THE LAND OF MORIAH. SACRIFICE HIM
> THERE AS A BURNT OFFERING ON ONE OF
> THE MOUNTAINS, WHICH I WILL
> POINT OUT TO YOU."
> *Genesis 22:1–2*

This Scripture always bothered me. *God, sometimes you expect way too much. I already surrendered my body to you. How much more do you want?* He showed me soon after my cancer treatment. My husband was terminated from his job. The timing couldn't have been worse. It was shortly after 9/11 and my business was also going through a slump. Through fourteen months of unemployment we struggled to gain control over our financial security. Finally we surrendered it to God's control. Slowly, I'm learning He wants more than my body and my finances. He wants all of me (Romans 12:1–2). He wants me to lay aside my own desires and trust Him to know what's best for me. He wants my intimate knowledge of His Word and His character to become my underlying foundation for living. He wants my obedience. He wants me to trust Him with my future. And He wants my heart. He wants me to love Him more than any activity, achievement, or relationship. *Even more than my husband and children?* Yes. He wants me to be wholly committed . . . totally and passionately sold out.

Thankfully, God doesn't expect this level of commitment from us all at once. Abraham obeyed God's instructions for thirty years before he carried out one of the greatest acts of obedience in history. During this time, he learned many tough lessons that deepened his character and ability to obey God. God first told him to venture out to a new land (Genesis 12:1). Abraham chose the uncertainty of traveling under God's direction over the security of His present situation. In this ultimate test, God wanted Abraham to sacrifice Isaac, his only child. Abraham trusted God's provision and carried out His instructions (Genesis 22:1–8). At the last minute, God sent an angel to stop him saying, "Lay down the knife. . . . For now I know that you truly fear God. You have not withheld even your beloved son from me" (Genesis 22:12). Abraham, his descendents, and all the nations of the earth received abundant blessings because Abraham obeyed God (Genesis 22:16–18).

Think of it. God spared Abraham's son but sacrificed His own for you and me. When we offer ourselves as living sacrifices out of gratitude for all Christ has done, God returns more than we could ever dream. The benefits of His blessing far outweigh any sacrifice we could ever make. So the next time God lights the pathway in front of your feet and you know exactly what He wants from you, obey immediately. He might start with simple things. *Go talk with your neighbor. Offer to pray for a friend.* When you obey, He'll light the path a little more and His next instruction will be clear. Don't expect Him to light up the whole runway. His timing is perfect. He knows your circumstances intimately. Little by little, He'll develop your character for greater tests. With each test will come greater love for God, a deeper knowledge of His ways, and more blessings than you can count. Before you know it, you're totally sold out. ❦

YOU HAVE HEARD THAT THE LAW OF MOSES
SAYS, "LOVE YOUR NEIGHBOR" AND HATE
YOUR ENEMY. BUT I SAY, LOVE YOUR
ENEMIES! PRAY FOR THOSE WHO PERSECUTE
YOU! IN THAT WAY, YOU WILL BE ACTING AS
TRUE CHILDREN OF YOUR FATHER IN
HEAVEN. FOR HE GIVES HIS SUNLIGHT TO
BOTH THE EVIL AND THE GOOD, AND HE
SENDS RAIN ON THE JUST AND ON THE
UNJUST, TOO. IF YOU LOVE ONLY THOSE
WHO LOVE YOU, WHAT GOOD IS THAT? EVEN
CORRUPT TAX COLLECTORS DO THAT
MUCH. IF YOU ARE KIND ONLY TO YOUR
FRIENDS, HOW ARE YOU DIFFERENT FROM
ANYONE ELSE? EVEN PAGANS DO THAT.
Matthew 5:43–47

Every person on this earth bears the image of God (Genesis 1:26). Your unfriendly neighbor, the guy who cut you off on the freeway this morning on your way to the clinic, the homeless man on the street corner, and the hardened felon who committed the most heinous of crimes—they're all image bearers. Each one is a person of worth in God's eyes, and Jesus commands us to love them in the same way that He loves us (John 15:12). His command to love extends beyond our friends to our enemies and those who persecute us. The apostle John said it's impossible to live in the light of Christ and hate a Christian brother or sister at the same time (1 John 2:9). If I claim to be a Christian but I don't love others, I don't really belong to God (1 John 3:10, 17). *But*

Lord, how do I love the person who spread lies about me and treated me so unfairly? How do I love the person who boasts constantly and never follows through on a commitment? How do I love the person who avoids me now that I have cancer? How do I love when I feel no love? How do I see them through your eyes?

What a relief to know that Christian love is not a feeling. I would fail miserably at love if left to my own resources. God doesn't expect me to *feel* love and affection for anyone I find difficult to love. He expects me to show His love through my actions purely out of obedience to Him. So instead of ignoring that boastful colleague or disliking that person who falsely criticized my motives, I can choose to treat them with kindness and respect. I can choose to put their needs before my own and expect nothing in return. When they annoy or offend me, I can choose to pray for them. An amazing thing happens when I choose to act in love: God uses me as a vessel to express His love. Right before my own eyes, my enemy transforms into the child God sees (1 John 2:10).

Perhaps you'll find out as I did that you can't love your enemies in your own power. As you draw closer to God, He'll start replacing your heart with His. God's character will be reflected in your love, patience, kindness, forgiveness, and faithfulness. Your growing relationship with Him will result in growing relationships with others. And when you choose to show love, you can be confident standing before the Lord, even if you *feel* no love, because God is greater than your heart and your feelings are no secret to Him (1 John 3:18–20). So the next time someone ruffles your feathers, choose to be kind. Choose to pray. Ask God to let you see your enemy through His eyes. The image bearer you see will amaze you! ❦

FROM ORDINARY TO EXTRAORDINARY

> THE MEMBERS OF THE COUNCIL WERE
> AMAZED WHEN THEY SAW THE BOLDNESS OF
> PETER AND JOHN, FOR THEY COULD SEE
> THAT THEY WERE ORDINARY MEN WHO HAD
> HAD NO SPECIAL TRAINING. THEY ALSO
> RECOGNIZED THEM AS MEN WHO
> HAD BEEN WITH JESUS.
> *Acts 4:13*

I'm just a little girl . . . the first-born daughter of a Dairy Queen owner from a small town in southern Minnesota. I had an ordinary childhood. I grew up in a stable home with a brother, a sister, and a golden retriever. My parents taught me hard work and responsibility. They made sure I was baptized, confirmed, and went to Sunday school. I earned a couple of college degrees, got married, had two kids, and got on with the business of living. I never dreamed I would lay hands on the sick and witness the Lord's healing power. I never imagined I would lead a ministry, serve as an elder in the body of Christ, or share the Gospel with the lost and hopeless. I knew absolutely nothing about Christian leadership until cancer brought me into the presence of Christ. My brokenness turned my occasional Bible dabbling into a serious hunger for the Word of God. It turned my rebellion into obedience. God used cancer to call an ordinary little girl to do extraordinary things for His kingdom. I have no special training . . . but I've been with Jesus.

Peter and John were ordinary men. They had no special training like the rulers, elders, and teachers of religious law who made up the Jewish high council did. Still, they spoke for God and presented the Good News of Jesus Christ with an authority and boldness that amazed the council. Even when the high council ordered them to stop, they could not keep quiet. These men had been with Christ. They could not stop telling the world about the wonderful things they had seen and heard (Acts 4:18–20).

As you spend more and more time in your Bible and with the Lord in prayer, you will light up the darkness around you. People will be amazed at your boldness. You may have cancer, but they see peace. You may have a discouraging test result, but they see hope. You may have every reason for despair, but they see joy. You can't help but tell the world of the wonderful things He has done for you. Your testimony will convince others of Christ's power.

So don't be surprised when God uses your cancer for His glory. You may be an ordinary person with no special training, but He will always equip you to do His work (Ephesians 4:11–12). Whether He gives you someone to mentor and encourage, or an entire ministry, your call will be extraordinary. And you have had the best training available . . . you've been with Jesus. ❦

GREAT TRIALS, GREAT PRAISE

> "LORD, HELP!" THEY CRIED IN THEIR
> TROUBLE, AND HE SAVED THEM FROM THEIR
> DISTRESS. HE SPOKE, AND THEY WERE
> HEALED—SNATCHED FROM THE DOOR OF
> DEATH. LET THEM PRAISE THE LORD FOR HIS
> GREAT LOVE AND FOR ALL HIS WONDERFUL
> DEEDS TO THEM. LET THEM OFFER
> SACRIFICES OF THANKSGIVING AND SING
> JOYFULLY ABOUT HIS GLORIOUS ACTS.
> *Psalm 107:19–22*

When the Lord snatched me from the door of death, it was hard to keep it all to myself. I wanted to shout praises to Him for His wonderful deeds, to tell my family, friends, and everyone I knew what He had done. But when I shared how the Lord healed me from cancer, I was troubled by how some people received my testimony. Some reacted with discomfort, others with doubt, and a few with offense. Over time, I have observed how cancer survivors and others who know heartbreak, grief, and brokenness have matured under adversity and often have a deep insight into God's love. Those who have not suffered a serious hardship may not always comprehend the depth of God's grace and mercy. They may not yet know their need for God or be ready to receive His message of hope.

The discomfort of some should not discourage our testimony. God wants us to tell everyone what He has done (Acts 1:8). Once we have a taste of walking in His will—when we have lived in His presence and have had a personal encounter with the living

Christ—we can't keep it to ourselves. God has given us a wonderful message to tell others. He has made us Christ's ambassadors. If we let Him, He can use the hardship of cancer to share His message of reconciliation with the world (2 Corinthians 5:18–20). We have been snatched from the door of death and redeemed by the blood of Jesus! What an awesome privilege to encourage others in their faith. How can we not be obedient to such a call?

So don't be discouraged when the Lord delivers you from cancer and your testimony falls on a few deaf ears. Once you have been in the throne room of God there's simply no turning back. Keep praying for those who refuse to listen and sharing your story with those who will. You will never be able to hide what the Lord has done for you. Great trials lead to great praise. ❦

> THERE WAS A MAN NAMED JABEZ WHO WAS
> MORE DISTINGUISHED THAN ANY OF HIS
> BROTHERS. HIS MOTHER NAMED HIM JABEZ
> BECAUSE HIS BIRTH HAD BEEN SO PAINFUL.
> HE WAS THE ONE WHO PRAYED TO THE GOD
> OF ISRAEL, "OH, THAT YOU WOULD BLESS
> ME AND EXTEND MY LANDS! PLEASE BE WITH
> ME IN ALL THAT I DO, AND KEEP ME FROM
> ALL TROUBLE AND PAIN!" AND GOD
> GRANTED HIM HIS REQUEST.
> *1 Chronicles 4:9–10*

When prayer ministers laid hands on me and prayed for healing early in my cancer, I was astounded by a blessing one man spoke over me. He asked the Lord to take my suffering and multiply it seven times in blessing. Wow. I never conceived I could ever be blessed that much. I knew the depth of my suffering. I couldn't imagine the equivalent in blessings multiplied sevenfold. *Oh, that God would bless me! I want to be free from cancer, free from trouble, and free from pain. I want you to open the windows of heaven and pour out blessings so great I won't have enough room to take it in! Lord, how can I know such blessing?*

Jabez simply prayed. He asked God to bless him, help him in his work, be with him always, and keep him safe. God granted Jabez's request because He loves to bless His people (Matthew 7:11).

Jesus also tells us how to be blessed. In the Sermon on the Mount, He described the values and traits of those who belong to

God. It's not always easy to be a Christ follower because God's way of living contradicts the world. The world rewards pride and personal independence, but God blesses those who realize their need for Him. The world rewards happiness at any cost, but God blesses those whose hope and joy are independent of outward circumstances. The world rewards power and success, but God blesses those who are humble and obedient (Matthew 5:3–5). God wants us to love when others hate, give when others take, help when others turn away, and give up our own rights to serve others. He has something very special in store for those who live out these values.

Do you desire blessings so great you won't have room to take them in? Then set your sights on heaven. Don't think only about the things here on earth (Colossians 3:2). The world's values are temporary, but God's values are eternal. Pray every day for blessing and protection, and strive to put God's priorities into daily practice. When you look at life through spiritual eyes and seek what God desires, you will walk in harmony with Him. He will take His rightful place as Lord of your health, Lord of your family, and Lord of your life. Before long the windows of heaven will open, and you'll be blessed beyond belief. ❦

> JESUS TOOK THE BLIND MAN BY THE HAND
> AND LED HIM OUT OF THE VILLAGE. THEN,
> SPITTING ON THE MAN'S EYES, HE LAID HIS
> HANDS ON HIM AND ASKED, "CAN YOU SEE
> ANYTHING NOW?" THE MAN LOOKED
> AROUND. "YES," HE SAID, "I SEE PEOPLE, BUT
> I CAN'T SEE THEM VERY CLEARLY. THEY
> LOOK LIKE TREES WALKING AROUND." THEN
> JESUS PLACED HIS HANDS OVER THE MAN'S
> EYES AGAIN. AS THE MAN STARED INTENTLY,
> HIS SIGHT WAS COMPLETELY RESTORED, AND
> HE COULD SEE EVERYTHING CLEARLY.
> *Mark 8:23–25*

We live in an instant world, and we are used to instant results. I can make dinner in five minutes with salad-in-a-bag and a microwave oven. I can get film developed and prescription eyeglasses made in less than an hour. Why wait for the U.S. mail when I can send a fax or an e-mail? Instant messenger, instant replay, instant coffee . . . instant healing? Cancer? Yes, it can happen in the spiritual realm. I know people who received prayer for a cancerous tumor and amazed the doctors when they showed up the next day for surgery and the tumor was gone. In the medical realm, however, it may take time to see the physical proof of what God has done. When I finished my treatment, I knew in my spirit that God had healed me. But the doctors wouldn't declare me cured. Test after test, year after year, the physical circumstances have gradually confirmed my healing.

Jesus healed the blind man in stages. First He laid hands on the man, and his sight was partially restored. When he placed His hands over the man's eyes again, his sight was completely restored, and he could see everything. Jesus laid hands on hundreds of people and healed them instantly. By healing the blind man in stages, He was likely showing us that sometimes healing is gradual rather than instantaneous.

Don't be discouraged if the physical manifestation of your healing comes slowly. Like the apostle Paul, you can find peace and contentment in God, not your doctor's report. Paul learned to rejoice whether he had plenty or little, whether his stomach was full or empty (Philippians 4:11–13). He knew his physical circumstances were not the source of true contentment. So rejoice while you wait! Be grateful for all the Lord has done for you. Stay faithful and keep reading your Bible. Pray for patience and ask Him to remove your doubts. He promises if you stay connected with Him you will produce much fruit (John 15:5). Humble yourself under God's mighty power and in His perfect time your healing will come (1 Peter 5:6). God's delays are not denials. ❦

JOY THAT LASTS FOREVER

> SO WE DON'T LOOK AT THE TROUBLES WE
> CAN SEE RIGHT NOW; RATHER, WE LOOK
> FORWARD TO WHAT WE HAVE NOT YET
> SEEN. FOR THE TROUBLES WE SEE WILL SOON
> BE OVER, BUT THE JOYS TO COME
> WILL LAST FOREVER.
> *2 Corinthians 4:18*

I remember when I was in labor with my firstborn son. After seventeen hours of exhausting contractions and still no baby, I was ready to pack my bags and go home. My husband reminded me there was no turning back. One way or another, the baby was coming and I had no choice but to deliver it! There were times during my cancer journey when I grew weary of the fight and wanted to quit. I wanted to get in the car and drive away. I didn't know where I would go, since I could have driven to the ends of the earth and the cancer would still be with me. Just as I had no choice but to deliver my son, I had no choice but to endure my cancer. Thank God He didn't leave me to my own resources. My weakness allowed the power of Christ to give me strength when I had no strength left. He pulled me out of the pit of despair and reminded me He had already defeated disease and suffering.

In the midst of chemo, baldness, fatigue, and an uncertain future, it's easy to focus on the pain. It's tempting to lose heart and quit. But I have learned there was a greater purpose in my suffering. My cancer forced me to depend on God. It humbled me and kept my pride in check. It tested my faith and allowed God to show His power (2 Corinthians 4:7). It focused my thoughts on eternal things and taught me just how brief this life on earth really is (2 Corinthians 4:12; Psalm 39:4). Most of all, it reminded me how Christ suffered and died so I could live with Him forever in a place where all sorrow and mourning will disappear (Isaiah 35:10). In my deepest despair, I tasted the joy of living in His presence.

Today, you may be so weary of chemo, wigs, and doctor visits that you want to run away. You and I are not the first to feel this way, and we won't be the last. When trouble and persecution wore down the apostle Paul, he looked up. He focused on the strength that comes from the Holy Spirit (Ephesians 3:16). He saw his troubles as opportunities for Christ to demonstrate His power and His presence. Think of it! Your very weakness allows the power of Christ to ease your pain and give you enough grace to face the next day (2 Corinthians 12:9–10). So don't let the weariness of your cancer force your eyes off Jesus and your eternal reward. Like labor pains, your troubles will soon be over. Your cancer journey won't last very long. But the joy it produces will last forever. 🦋

WHY, LORD?

> "TEACHER," HIS DISCIPLES ASKED HIM, "WHY
> WAS THIS MAN BORN BLIND? WAS IT A
> RESULT OF HIS OWN SINS OR THOSE OF HIS
> PARENTS?" "IT WAS NOT BECAUSE OF HIS
> SINS OR HIS PARENTS' SINS," JESUS
> ANSWERED. "HE WAS BORN BLIND SO THE
> POWER OF GOD COULD BE SEEN IN HIM."
> *John 9:2–3*

I dared not ask the obvious questions that occasionally rose from the depths of my soul. *Why, Lord? Did I eat the wrong foods or take the wrong drugs? Did I work too hard and relax too little? Was it too much stress and not enough sleep? Is it hereditary? Will I pass it on to my daughter? Why did you let this happen? Am I being punished for something I did? Something my parents did? Something their parents did? How does breast cancer happen to a healthy forty-seven-year-old woman with no family history of cancer, healthy parents, and grandparents who lived to their eighties and nineties?* I knew better than to ask. I knew asking would take my eyes off Jesus and cast doubt on His sovereignty and His love for me. I knew it could throw me into a downward spiral of fear and distrust. Still . . . I couldn't help wondering.

The disciples wondered too. Suffering was considered a result of sin in Jewish culture. They wondered if the man's blindness was the result of his sin or the sin of his parents. But Jesus said the man was born blind so the power of God could be demonstrated through him. He used the blind man's suffering to teach about faith and to bring glory to God. Jesus restored the man's sight. As the man began to experience God's grace through his new eye-sight, his spiritual eyes were opened as well. He recognized Jesus as the Son of God (John 9:38). As a result of his suffering, he came to know Christ.

Yes, we live in a fallen world where innocent people some-times suffer. What a comfort to know God can bring good out of any suffering, no matter how painful (Romans 8:28). Sure, you might wonder why this cancer happened. You might even wonder where you went wrong. But before you find yourself grumbling and complaining from the pit of despair, seek God. Ask Him to give you the strength to endure. Ask for a clearer understanding of what's happening and what He wants you to learn from it. Ask that your cancer would bring honor to His name. Regardless of the reason for your cancer God can use it to demonstrate His power and bring glory to His Son. You may ask, "Why, Lord?" To bring you into His presence and close to His heart . . . closer than you ever could have come without it. ❦

A Sister's Heart

> GOD HAS GIVEN EACH OF US THE ABILITY TO
> DO CERTAIN THINGS WELL. SO IF GOD HAS
> GIVEN YOU THE ABILITY TO PROPHESY,
> SPEAK OUT WHEN YOU HAVE FAITH THAT
> GOD IS SPEAKING THROUGH YOU. IF YOUR
> GIFT IS THAT OF SERVING OTHERS, SERVE
> THEM WELL. IF YOU ARE A TEACHER, DO A
> GOOD JOB OF TEACHING. IF YOUR GIFT IS TO
> ENCOURAGE OTHERS, DO IT! IF YOU HAVE
> MONEY, SHARE IT GENEROUSLY. IF GOD HAS
> GIVEN YOU LEADERSHIP ABILITY, TAKE THE
> RESPONSIBILITY SERIOUSLY. AND IF YOU
> HAVE A GIFT FOR SHOWING KINDNESS TO
> OTHERS, DO IT GLADLY.
> *Romans 12:6–8*

My sister has always had a servant's heart. There was the time she brought a young nephew into her home to live when his parents couldn't care for him. And the time she gave a woman from our hometown a place to stay while her husband lay in critical condition in the hospital. It was my sister who sat at the feet of a frightened old woman in a cruise ship restaurant and comforted her after she nearly choked on her dinner. And it was my sister who got chemo duty. She took off work, drove eighty miles one way, and stayed with me through every session. She brought me food, kept me company, and made darn sure I was cared for properly. Others offered, but I wanted my sister. She has the gift of serving.

God has given each of us different gifts to serve Him. One

person can't possibly embody all these gifts and one gift is not superior to another. Some have the gift of compassion while others encourage. Some are givers and others are leaders. Some prophesy, some teach, and others serve. Our spiritual gifts are not for our own advancement. We are to be faithful and serve Him with the gifts He has given us to build up the church. Together, we can carry out God's work more fully than any of us could do alone (Romans 12:1–11).

The Christian friends and family who come to your aid during your cancer journey are united in their love for one another and for the Lord (Ephesians 4:16). You might be amazed at how God has gifted them. Some may help research your treatment options and help facilitate your conversations with your doctor. Some will show compassion and kindness, praying with you in your distress. Some may encourage you when your faith is wavering. Others offer comfort by speaking God's Word into your heart. Servants like my sister will quickly take the initiative to help you with your practical needs. Together, they are a reflection of God's perfect love. Together, they form the head, heart, hands, and feet of Christ. Through them, you have seen Jesus. ❦

A Brother's Encouragement

CARRY EACH OTHER'S BURDENS, AND IN
THIS WAY YOU WILL FULFILL
THE LAW OF CHRIST.
Galatians 6:2 NIV

*M*y brother is a man of few words. There is no mistaking his Scandinavian heritage. But deep down inside that tough exterior is a tender heart. During my cancer, I found out how tender. He called every week without fail to check on me during chemo. He asked how things were going when sometimes my own family forgot to ask. He reminded me to rest and take care of myself. He scolded me when I pushed too hard. His kind words of concern helped carry the burden of my cancer.

God sends people to encourage those in need. Jethro encouraged Moses and gave him wise counsel when he was wearing himself out resolving disputes among the Israelites (Exodus 18:13–23). Paul experienced hardship all his Christian life, but God sustained him by sending godly friends. Timothy, Mark, and Luke encouraged and supported him when he was a lonely prisoner in a damp and chilly dungeon (2 Timothy 4:9–11). God calls us to be devoted to each other in brotherly love and take delight in honoring each other. When others are happy, be happy with them. When they are sad, share in their sorrow (Romans 12:10, 15). The kind words and actions of friends and loved ones can strengthen and bring comfort when we suffer. Their very presence sustains us in our distress.

Jesus said the world would know those who belong to Him by

the love we show to one another (John 13:35). When God comforts you in your sorrow, He will always send someone to share your burden. Whom has God sent to encourage you during these dark days when you can see no end to chemo, radiation, nausea, and fatigue? It could be a brother or sister, a neighbor or close friend. It may be that God has been planning all along to make you into the kind of person who will carry the burdens of others. Let others carry your load today. Someday soon, when this cancer ordeal is over, you can carry theirs. ❦

A MOTHER'S GRIEF

> WHEN MARY ARRIVED AND SAW JESUS, SHE
> FELL DOWN AT HIS FEET AND SAID, "LORD, IF
> YOU HAD BEEN HERE, MY BROTHER WOULD
> NOT HAVE DIED." WHEN JESUS SAW HER
> WEEPING AND SAW THE OTHER PEOPLE
> WAILING WITH HER, HE WAS MOVED WITH
> INDIGNATION AND WAS DEEPLY TROUBLED.
> "WHERE HAVE YOU PUT HIM?" HE ASKED
> THEM. THEY TOLD HIM, "LORD, COME
> AND SEE." THEN JESUS WEPT.
> *John 11:32–35*

The most difficult person to tell was my mother. Maybe it was because I'm a mother myself. I understand the dull ache I feel in my heart when my children suffer. I want to take all their pain upon myself. I want to suffer in their place. I understand a mother's grief. How could I tell this mother of three that her first-born daughter had cancer? At first we were optimistic. The tumor was small and cancer had not likely moved past the breast. But when the surgeon confirmed my positive nodes, the news broke my mother's heart.

Jesus understands every emotion my mother felt that day. When Lazarus died and He saw Mary and the others weeping and wailing, He was moved with compassion and indignation. Then Jesus wept too. Even though He would later raise Lazarus from the dead, He shared in their grief. The Son of God cared enough to weep with them in their sorrow. He also grieved their hopelessness when they had every reason for hope. Here He stood, the Resurrection and the Life, right under their noses (John 11:25–44).

As followers of Christ, we are never left on our own to grieve. Jesus is always with us, and with Him there is always hope. We have hope because God can bring good out of any situation (Romans 8:28). We have hope because nothing in all creation, not cancer or death or all the powers of heaven and hell can ever separate us from His love (Romans 8:38–39). We have hope because Jesus suffered in our place so we can live with Him forever in eternity (John 3:16).

Being a Christian won't exempt us from grief and suffering. Jesus said we would have trouble. But by His death and resurrection, He overcame the world (John 16:33). By His death and resurrection, He conquered your cancer. The risen Christ is your hope and comfort. Those who have been ransomed by Him will sing songs of everlasting joy. Sorrow and mourning will disappear and they will be overcome with joy and gladness (Isaiah 51:11). "He will rise with healing in his wings. And you will go free, leaping with joy like calves let out to pasture" (Malachi 4:2). Now that's good news for mothers everywhere. ❦

A FATHER'S PRAYERS

HE PRAYED MORE FERVENTLY, AND HE WAS
IN SUCH AGONY OF SPIRIT THAT HIS SWEAT
FELL TO THE GROUND LIKE GREAT DROPS
OF BLOOD.
Luke 22:44

My dad is the picture of perfect health . . . a man in his seventies with the body of a forty-year-old. He swims laps for an hour each day. And while he swims, he prays. He prays for an extended time each morning too. He prayed for me throughout my cancer journey. He prays for others battling sickness and disease. Not shallow prayer, but deep intercessory prayer that only a few will ever experience.

God looks for people who will stand in the gap, whose hearts are prepared to be intercessors before Him (Ezekiel 22:30). He looks for those who are bold and committed and have hearts in tune with His. They are willing to go before Him and seek mercy and compassion for the sinner and the sick and pray as long as necessary to obtain an answer . . . until they know in their spirit that their prayers have broken through every barrier. He is looking for those who will pray at such a deep level that their heart grieves and their entire body agonizes for those for whom they are interceding (Hebrews 5:7). They will stay before God when everyone else has gone away or fallen sleep . . . as Jesus prayed in the garden.

Yes, deep prolonged intercession is painful. But there are certain blessings of God that simply won't come to pass until someone prays them in. The Lord himself came into the world through intercession. Simeon and Anna were prayer warriors who fasted and prayed day and night for years for the Messiah to come. They rejoiced when they recognized baby Jesus in the temple as their long-awaited Savior (Luke 2:25–32; 36–38). Their prayers had been answered.

Most people don't commit voluntarily to this level of prayer. God calls His intercessors, and it's a lonely business. There may be days, months, or years when no results come. They may never see the receipt for their efforts in this earthly life, but God's Word *never* comes back empty—it always produces fruit (Isaiah 55:11).

If you don't have a personal intercessor, ask God to help you find someone willing to pray through your cancer until healing comes. Perhaps because you've shared their pain, God has called you to intercede for others suffering cancer. Take your call seriously. You might be the only one standing between a sick person and their healing. You might want to take up swimming. 🌿

The Place of Surrender

> This left Jacob all alone in the camp,
> and a man came and wrestled with him
> until dawn. When the man saw that he
> couldn't win the match, he struck
> Jacob's hip and knocked it out of joint
> at the socket. Then the man said, "Let
> me go, for it is dawn." But Jacob
> panted, "I will not let you go
> unless you bless me."
> *Genesis 32:24–26*

Jacob feared the reunion with his older brother Esau. It had been twenty years since he had stolen Esau's family blessing and his right as a firstborn son to the family inheritance. Esau was so angry, he had threatened to kill Jacob as soon as their father, Isaac, died (Genesis 25:29–27:42). And now it was time to face his brother. Jacob was so terrified he turned to God for mercy (Genesis 32:1–12).

Jacob had a history of controlling and manipulating and solving problems his own way. But this time he knew God was his only hope. He wanted God's blessing so badly that he wouldn't let go of the angel God sent. So the angel dislocated Jacob's hip. It was the only way God could overcome his strong will. Finally, Jacob reached a place of complete brokenness and surrender. He would no longer walk in his own strength. He would now walk with a limp, symbolizing his dependence on God alone. God could now bless Jacob abundantly with the inheritance He had promised long before (Genesis 28:13–15). God restored his relationship with Esau and made Jacob the father of the twelve tribes of Israel.

I can relate to Jacob. Perhaps you can too. I like doing things my own way. I'm pretty good at it. I don't like to admit I can be controlling or manipulative, but my family would agree I certainly can be strong-willed! I've achieved earthly success through self-effort, but God had an awesome plan for my life that I would never come to know until I fully surrendered to Him and let Him take the lead. Breast cancer was my dislocated hip. It brought me to a place of brokenness. It brought me to my knees where I am fully dependent on God alone. And every day since it keeps me there . . . seeking His face and His will.

Perhaps this cancer is a time of preparation for you too. Perhaps God is using this time to change your old nature and bring you into total dependence on Him. Only God knows what is best for you. When you trust Him with all your heart and seek His will in all you do, your life can become exactly the way He intended it to be . . . healthy, vital, fruitful, and prosperous (Proverbs 3:5–7, Psalm 1). Let God take you from the place of surrender to the place of blessing He planned all along. ❦

IF YOU NEED WISDOM—IF YOU WANT TO
KNOW WHAT GOD WANTS YOU TO DO—ASK
HIM, AND HE WILL GLADLY TELL YOU. HE
WILL NOT RESENT YOUR ASKING. BUT WHEN
YOU ASK HIM, BE SURE THAT YOU REALLY
EXPECT HIM TO ANSWER, FOR A DOUBTFUL
MIND IS AS UNSETTLED AS A WAVE OF THE
SEA THAT IS DRIVEN AND TOSSED BY THE
WIND. PEOPLE LIKE THAT SHOULD NOT
EXPECT TO RECEIVE ANYTHING FROM THE
LORD. THEY CAN'T MAKE UP THEIR MINDS.
THEY WAVER BACK AND FORTH IN
EVERYTHING THEY DO.

James 1:5–8

Decisions, decisions. First it's the surgery. Lumpectomy or mastectomy? For some, it's what type of reconstruction. Implant or skin flap? Each has its own range of options. Then it's the chemo. Clinical trial or standard treatment? Even radiation comes with a set of choices. And if that's not enough, when the chemo and radiation are over, it's time to think prevention. Another decision to make. There was the standard widely prescribed hormone therapy for post-breast cancer treatment. And there was another option with far fewer side effects, but no FDA approval for breast cancer prevention. My oncologist was "comfortable" prescribing this alternative drug for the next five years. He believed the research was solid. Was I? It was my choice. *Lord, am I comfortable? What should I do?*

I did what I always did when faced with a thousand different breast cancer choices. I prayed. When we ask Him, God will give us the ability to make wise decisions in the midst of the most difficult circumstances. He always supplies exactly what we need (Philippians 4:19). When I pray, I expect God will hear and I always trust He will answer. Then, when the answer comes deep in my spirit, I can be confident it comes from God. In this case, His answer was counter to common practice. The alternative I chose was somewhat controversial in the world's view. But this was not the time to second guess and look backward (Luke 9:62).

We simply can't approach God with a doubtful, wavering mind. To do so puts His counsel at the same level as everyone else's. It allows me to choose between God's Word, the world's perspective, or even my own emotions. And I can't pick and choose and follow Him selectively. He wants my wholehearted commitment, my total dedication, and my total trust.

Yes, the choices you face throughout your breast cancer journey can be overwhelming. What a relief to know you don't have to stumble around in the darkness searching for the right thing to do. Commit yourself wholly and completely to God for the answers you need. He always has your best interests at heart. Your Creator knows your body better than any doctor, and He knows what the future will bring. So if you need wisdom, if you want to know what God wants you to do, simply ask. But be sure that you really expect Him to answer. When the answer comes, ask God to settle the waves of doubt that may be tossing and turning in the depths of your soul. You can be comfortable when the answers you seek come directly from heaven. Need wisdom? Pray! ❦

WARRIOR PRINCESS

AS IRON SHARPENS IRON, A FRIEND
SHARPENS A FRIEND.
Proverbs 27:17

I have girl friends. We're a group of four women who meet every week to love, encourage, and pray for each other. Through our laughter and our tears, we challenge each other to become all that God intended for us to become. We hold each other accountable to stay connected with Christ through regular Bible study and prayer and do the right thing in our Christian walk. We jokingly call ourselves "warrior princesses" because together we are striving to live like daughters of the King in a fallen and broken world.

It wasn't always this way. Before my breast cancer, I thought all I needed was my husband and a family who loved me. Perhaps I was afraid of letting anyone get too close. They might learn what was under that perfect exterior, and they might not like it. I resisted for years when our church strongly promoted small groups and the importance of biblical community. *I can hold myself accountable, thank you.* Perhaps that's why my spiritual growth remained stagnant for so long.

God never intended for believers to live in isolation. Even His Son had close friends. His friends weren't perfect, but they had hearts set on following God. He wants the same for us. He wants us to be surrounded by those who call on the Lord with pure hearts (2 Timothy 2:22). He knows we will face difficulty in this life, and He never planned for us to face it alone. We can find strength, comfort, and support when other believers help carry our burdens (Galatians 6:2). He also knows we are in constant danger of falling off the path He intended us to walk. We can trust those who are seeking God's will, who love and support us and know us intimately, to hold us accountable when we fall into temptation (James 5:19–20). They are willing to tell us the truth and even risk hurting our feelings because they have our best interests at heart (Proverbs 27:6).

If breast cancer caught you with a solid foundation of close personal Christian relationships, you are blessed. As iron sharpens iron, let them challenge you to grow spiritually and draw closer to Christ. If, like me, you were caught without a small group of Christian woman who love and encourage you, take heart. Ask God to put people you can trust to form such deep relationships in your path. Your faith community may assist in bringing those with common interests together to meet regularly, study the Bible, and pray for each other. Perhaps through breast cancer, God started a refining work in your heart. A small group of friends who love you and love Jesus can help Him complete it. They can help you become the warrior princess God planned all along. ❦

LET THERE BE TEARS

DRAW CLOSE TO GOD, AND GOD WILL
DRAW CLOSE TO YOU. WASH YOUR HANDS,
YOU SINNERS; PURIFY YOUR HEARTS, YOU
HYPOCRITES. LET THERE BE TEARS FOR THE
WRONG THINGS YOU HAVE DONE. LET
THERE BE SORROW AND DEEP GRIEF.

James 4:8–9

*G*od has promised a life of joy, but we can't begin to experience it until we come to terms with our sin. There was a time when pride kept me from viewing myself as a *sinner*. After all, I was a good wife and mother. I worked hard. I didn't steal, murder, or cheat on my husband. It was not until the sorrow of my cancer brought me into deep study of the Bible that I started to understand the depth and seriousness of my sin. As I read about the rebellious Israelites throughout the Old Testament, I finally began to comprehend the nature of human sin compared to the holiness and righteousness of our perfect God. Every time I do what I want to do, instead of what God wants me to do, I sin. Every time I talk behind someone's back, I sin. Every time I lose patience in traffic, I sin. It's my sin that separates me from God. It's my sin that caused the death of Jesus. It's my sin and yours, for we *all* fall short of God's glorious standard (Romans 3:23).

We fall short because God is righteous. God can do anything He wants because He's sovereign. He's God. We don't deserve anything, yet He wants to give us everything. We are unworthy of His love, but He loves us anyway . . . a love so extravagant, it knows no boundaries. So much love that He sent His Son to take our punishment. It was the sorrow of my sin that finally helped me understand the depth of God's grace and how badly I needed a Savior. God meets me exactly where I am. I don't have to clean up my act first. He forgives me and restores my relationship with Him simply because I ask with a repentant heart.

It's possible to be sorry for our sin and run away from God in shame instead of into His arms. Just look at Judas. He hung himself after betraying the Son of God for a few silver coins, and he went to his grave filled with sorrow and bitterness (Matthew 27:3–5). Peter betrayed Jesus too. Three times, in fact. But when he was fishing and spotted his risen Lord on the shore, he jumped into the water and swam *to* Him. He returned to Jesus, broken and remorseful, and reaffirmed his love for Him (John 21:7, 15–17). Peter's heart was repentant and God forgave him. He went on to preach boldly and experience the joy of seeing thousands respond to the Gospel message.

Like Peter, we will never be completely healed and made whole in Christ until our hearts break over our sin. Jesus said those who mourn would find comfort (Matthew 5:4). Those who grieve will draw close to God. Ask the Holy Spirit to reveal the depths of your human sin and the true character of God. Let there be tears for the wrong things you have done. They won't last long. When you come before Him with a truly repentant heart, He forgives your sins and never remembers them again (Hebrews 8:12). Let His comfort and joy overflow. ❦

SURRENDER ALL

THEN JESUS SAID TO THE DISCIPLES, "IF ANY
OF YOU WANTS TO BE MY FOLLOWER, YOU
MUST PUT ASIDE YOUR SELFISH AMBITION,
SHOULDER YOUR CROSS, AND FOLLOW ME.
IF YOU TRY TO KEEP YOUR LIFE FOR
YOURSELF, YOU WILL LOSE IT. BUT IF YOU
GIVE UP YOUR LIFE FOR ME, YOU WILL
FIND TRUE LIFE."
Matthew 16:24–25

I've heard lifeguards are trained to wait until their victims stop
trying to save themselves before attempting a rescue. If the
lifeguard attempts to save a victim who is still thrashing around in
a panic, there is a danger both will be pulled under the water and
drown. In the weeks before my diagnosis, I was drowning. But I
was downright determined to save myself. I would research myself
out of this mess. If I learned every single fact about breast cancer,
I could convince myself my symptoms didn't fit. And if that didn't
work, I would rationalize it away. *It simply isn't happening. It's all a
big mistake. I'm healthy. There's no breast cancer in my family.* I fought
kicking and screaming until the day before the doctor called with
the biopsy results. I finally stopped fighting for my life and let the
Lifeguard take over. I picked up my cross and started following
Jesus, and I haven't looked back since.

Gradually, in the months and years that followed, I've learned
He wants more than my health. The disciples knew shouldering
their cross to follow Jesus meant full surrender and no turning
back. He wants my full surrender too. He wants me to put all my

resources at His disposal and trust Him to guide every step (Romans 12:1). He wants me to surrender my family and friends, my career and ambitions, my reputation, my possessions, my social life, and my daily schedule. Most important, He wants my will. Paul said, "I die daily" (1 Corinthians 15:31 KJV). There isn't a day that goes by where I don't have to make a conscious decision to lay down my own desires and surrender my will to God. As I gradually let go of my own will and my worldly desires, He keeps showing me how good and pleasing and perfect *His* will really is (Romans 12:2). I'm slowly learning God has a much better plan for every area of my life than anything I could dream up on my own.

If you're still thrashing around in a panic trying to save yourself, be still (Psalm 46:10). Let the Lifeguard come to your rescue. Surrender your health and healing to Jesus. Let Him guide every step of your cancer recovery. Give Him authority over your doctors, your treatments, your body, and your mind. But when you pick up your cross, don't be surprised if there's no turning back. When you give up your life to follow Him, He promises to give you back the best He has to offer, in this world and the next. So surrender all! Let God transform your heart and your mind. Let Him show you His will and His perfect plans. Soon you'll be living the victorious life you were born to live! ❦

NOW IS THE TIME

I SAID, "PLANT THE GOOD SEEDS OF
RIGHTEOUSNESS, AND YOU WILL HARVEST A
CROP OF MY LOVE. PLOW UP THE HARD
GROUND OF YOUR HEARTS, FOR NOW IS THE
TIME TO SEEK THE LORD, THAT HE MAY
COME AND SHOWER RIGHTEOUSNESS
UPON YOU."

Hosea 10:12

My husband's parents were farmers in southern Minnesota. Every fall after harvest, my father-in-law would plow up the fields to prepare the hardened and packed earth for planting the next spring. I remember the look and smell of the freshly loosened black soil when it was finally ready to receive the corn or soybean seeds and the spring rains that would give life to the crops. Like hardened fields, the people in the northern kingdom of Israel had hardened hearts toward God. They had grown apathetic to His love and turned to idolatry. But God's love is constant and persistent. He spoke through the prophet Hosea that He would soften their hardened hearts. As my father-in-law plowed his fields to receive the seed and rain, God would break up the sinful barriers that kept His Word from penetrating. Then they would be able to seek Him again so He could shower them with righteousness.

I was a lot like the people of the northern kingdom. Cancer caught me with a hardened heart toward God. Other than my Sunday morning church ritual, I was fairly indifferent to His call on the rest of my life. My heart was focused on things of this world rather than things of God. I didn't read my Bible regularly and my prayer life was superficial. Until my diagnosis, God's Word couldn't always penetrate the barrier of my hardened heart. He used my cancer to break up the unplowed ground so I could seek Him and receive forgiveness for my indifference. My hardened heart became a plowed field, carefully prepared and ready for planting. God promises that when His Word penetrates deep into our heart, it brings life and radiant health (Proverbs 4:21–22). We'll never slip from our path and we'll have new power to live for Him (Psalm 37:31; 2 Corinthians 3:3). His Word gave me everything I needed to cope with months of chemo, hair loss, doubts, and fears. It gave me hope, peace, and the joy of restoration when the world offered nothing but uncertainty.

God never stops pursuing us. We can ignore Him for a lifetime, and He still forgives us when we turn to Him. His love knows no bounds and His compassion never fails (Hosea 14:3–8). If cancer caught you with a hardened heart, seek the Lord. Let your suffering plow up the hard ground and seek His forgiveness. When your heart is prepared and ready, the Word of God can penetrate as a plowed field soaks up seed and rain. Don't wait any longer. Now is the time. Let His righteousness rain down on you and harvest a bumper crop of love. 🌾

The Winds and Waves Obey Him

> The disciples woke him up, shouting,
> "Master, Master, we're going to
> drown!" So Jesus rebuked the wind and
> the raging waves. The storm stopped
> and all was calm! Then he asked them,
> "Where is your faith?" And they were
> filled with awe and amazement. They
> said to one another, "Who is this man,
> that even the winds and waves
> obey him?"
> *Luke 8:24–25*

When terrorists fly airplanes into buildings and kill thousands of innocent people, it's easy to wonder. When we pick up the newspaper and read about the victims of a violent crime, or see pictures of hungry children in war-torn third-world countries, it's easy to wonder. When healthy wives, mothers, daughters, and sisters get breast cancer, it's easy to wonder. We wonder if God has somehow lost control of the universe and we are all at the mercy of fate. Even the disciples wondered. Here they are in the middle of a fierce raging storm with God himself in the boat, convinced they would drown.

The disciples forgot how big their God is. They forgot He has supreme unlimited power over the entire universe. After all, He created it. History itself belongs to Him (Psalm 105). If you're still wondering, read a little from Psalm 104:

You placed the world on its foundation so it would never be

moved. You clothed the earth with floods of water, water that covered even the mountains. At the sound of your rebuke, the water fled; at the sound of your thunder, it fled away. Mountains rose and valleys sank to the levels you decreed. Then you set a firm boundary for the seas, so they would never again cover the earth. You make the springs pour water into ravines, so streams gush down from the mountains. They provide water for all the animals, and the wild donkeys quench their thirst. The birds nest beside the streams and sing among the branches of the trees. You send rain on the mountains from your heavenly home, and you fill the earth with the fruit of your labor. You cause grass to grow for the cattle. You cause plants to grow for people to use. You allow them to produce food from the earth—wine to make them glad, olive oil as lotion for their skin, and bread to give them strength. (Psalm 104:5–15)

God creates, orders, maintains, and governs. He controls everything and He is present everywhere. Heaven is His throne and the earth is His footstool (Isaiah 66:1). Our very breath depends on the life He breathed into us (Genesis 2:7; Job 33:4). If He were to take back His Spirit and withdraw His breath, all humanity would turn to dust (Job 34:14–15). Yet, in all His awesome power and majesty, He created you and me only a little lower than himself (Psalm 8:5). We bear the image of our Creator (Genesis 1:26–27). And He gave us authority over everything He made (Psalm 8:6).

Think of it. The same God who placed the world on its foundation—the same God who has faithfully ordered and maintained it since creation—this same God delights in you! And the God who made you will never fail you (1 Peter 4:19). He wants the very best for you. Nothing is too difficult for Him (Jeremiah

32:27). So you can stop wondering if He still controls the heavens and the earth or if the wind and waves still obey Him. The Lord is in the boat with you. And if He can calm the forces of nature, He can certainly calm the raging storm of your cancer. ❦

GOD PLEASER

OBVIOUSLY, I'M NOT TRYING TO BE A
PEOPLE PLEASER! NO, I AM TRYING TO
PLEASE GOD. IF I WERE STILL TRYING TO
PLEASE PEOPLE, I WOULD NOT BE
CHRIST'S SERVANT.
Galatians 1:10

*B*reast cancer gave no thought to my busy social schedule and the importance of my personal image. In the first few weeks of losing my hair, I had to give a bridal shower, attend a family wedding, and lead a training session, as well as hold numerous client meetings. Plus, Christmas was coming and it was my turn to host. With some help from my family and a good wig, I managed to pull it all off and still maintain my dignity. Winter gave me a little reprieve. No one questions hats in the winter, and I only scheduled things on good days. But as the weather warmed up, I had a son graduate from college, a daughter graduate from high school, two graduation parties to host, and my parents' fiftieth wedding anniversary. It was getting too hot for the wig, and baseball caps just weren't appropriate. What will people think? What will they think if I burn the roast, run out of food, or my wig falls into the fruit salad? What will they think if I toast my parents in front of two hundred people in a really bad crew cut?

All these "public appearances" brought me face-to-face with how important it was for me to please people and gain their approval. Paul said our purpose should be to please God, not people, for He is the one who examines the motives of our hearts (1 Thessalonians 2:4). God is not impressed with my perfect entertaining, perfect business services, or perfect appearance if I'm doing it all to bring glory to myself. But when my actions are motivated by love for Christ, He gets all the glory (1 Corinthians 10:31). If I focus on pleasing God, the needs of my loved ones will automatically be met. It is His will for me to love my family and friends, serve their needs, and put their interests before my own.

Sometimes our desire to please others compromises what we know God wants us to do. There are times when God has prompted me to pray with a friend over lunch or offer prayer for a family member going through a tough time. But I've held back, more concerned about what they might think than what pleases God. Occasionally I've been involved in conversations that I know are contrary to God's will, but I've gone along to keep from appearing overly righteous. Paul warned us not to copy the behavior and customs of this world, but to let God transform our minds so we always know what pleases Him (Romans 12:1).

Whom do you live to please? Husband? Parents? Children? Employer? Neighbors? Friends? We can't serve Christ faithfully if we're always worried about what everyone thinks of us. Seek His approval above everyone else's. He gives wisdom, knowledge, and joy to all who please Him (Ecclesiastes 2:26). And He doesn't care if you have a bad hair day or spots on the silverware. He will make your innocence as clear as the dawn and the justice of your cause will shine like the noonday sun (Psalm 37:5–6). Be a God pleaser! 🌿

THE FURNACE OF SUFFERING

HE WILL SIT AND JUDGE LIKE A REFINER OF
SILVER, WATCHING CLOSELY AS THE DROSS IS
BURNED AWAY. HE WILL PURIFY THE
LEVITES, REFINING THEM LIKE GOLD OR
SILVER, SO THAT THEY MAY ONCE AGAIN
OFFER ACCEPTABLE SACRIFICES
TO THE LORD.
Malachi 3:3

A wise Christian mentor told me at the beginning of my cancer journey that I was about to enter the refining fire. *Now* that *doesn't sound good!* As I lived through the fiery furnace of suffering, I slowly began to understand her words. Joseph went through the refining fire when he was sold into slavery and spent years in an Egyptian prison. David went through it after he was anointed king, spending years hiding in caves and running for his life. Paul went through it on the road to Damascus. Countless servants of God went through the fire before they did, and countless have gone through it since. Now it was my turn.

What does it mean that God will sit as a refiner and purifier of silver? In the silver refining process, the silversmith heats the raw metal in the middle of the fire where the flames are the hottest. The silver melts and the impurities rise to the surface. The silversmith skims the impurities off the top, leaving pure metal. Throughout the process of heating and melting, the silversmith never leaves the silver unattended. If left in the fire a moment too long, the silver is destroyed. Finally, when the reflection of the silversmith appears in the clear pure surface of the silver, the process is complete.

Yes, it was hot in the furnace. But the Silversmith never left my side. He never left me unattended, and He made sure the process didn't destroy me. The fire purified me like silver melted in a crucible. It refined my character and gave me deeper insight into His nature. It helped me understand my life is a gift and never a right to be taken for granted. It took me from a place of surrender to a place of great blessing and abundance (Psalm 66:10–12). Just as Joseph, David, Paul, and the Levite priests were purified and made acceptable before God, I discovered the fiery furnace of breast cancer strengthened my faith and prepared me for His call on my life (1 Peter 1:6–7). And ever so slowly, the reflection people see in the purified silver is beginning to resemble the Silversmith.

Are you being refined in the furnace of suffering? Be still, you have nothing to fear. The fire will get hot, but the Silversmith won't let you burn. He'll never leave you unattended. Turn to Him in faith and He'll give you strength to endure the heat. He'll gently remove all the impurities until you're strong in character and ready for anything (James 1:2–4). When the process is over, His reflection will shine so brightly everyone will want to stand in your light. ❦

BE STILL

> BE STILL, AND KNOW THAT I AM GOD; I WILL
> BE EXALTED AMONG THE NATIONS, I WILL BE
> EXALTED IN THE EARTH.
> *Psalm 46:10* NIV

Be still, and know that I am God. The words scrolled slowly across my computer screen saver. Even before my relationship with the Lord became more intimate, I found comfort in those words. When things got a little crazy in my business, or when life threw a curve ball of some sort, those words scrolling across my screen were always a good reminder that someone else was in charge. But this time was different. Be still? *There's a suspicious area on your left breast, but don't worry, it's probably nothing. Can you come back in a couple of weeks for a mammogram and an ultrasound?* Be still? *Mmmmm . . . the mammogram is negative, but the ultrasound is cause for concern. We'll have to schedule a biopsy. Can you come back in a week?* Be still? *We won't know the results of your biopsy until next Monday. Have a good weekend!* Be still? You've got to be kidding.

There are times in our Christian walk when we find ourselves in a place of waiting—waiting for test results, waiting for doctors, waiting for blood counts to rise, waiting for the next round of chemo, waiting for the next day of radiation—*waiting for the whole nightmare to be over.* When we are in this place of waiting, there is nothing we can do to change the situation. Nothing in our past experience matters. Our health history, our family health history, our record of good deeds or bad . . . none of it matters. Our inner voice screams *Do something!* into the eerie silence. But God says,

"Be still. Be still and know that I am God."

If we're obedient to God's voice and draw close to Him in this place of waiting, our roots can penetrate deeply into the soil of His perfect love. He'll show us His love is wide and long and high and deep enough to reach every corner of the silence (Ephesians 3:17–18). From His unlimited resources, He'll give us all the strength we need to endure (Ephesians 3:16). The silence won't last forever. The nightmare will end. He will leave us in this quiet place only for a season (Ecclesiastes 3:1). If we give Him all our worries and cares and humble ourselves under His mighty power, He will honor us in His good time (1 Peter 5:6–7).

Breast cancer may take you to this place of silence. You watch as the world around you continues to spin and the people continue living their lives. But your world has stopped. It may seem God has built a wall around you, and there is nothing but silence, nothing but waiting. Listen . . . can you hear His voice in the silence? He is calling you into a closer relationship with Him. He is calling you deeper into prayer and His Word. He wants you to know that when the world strips everything away and only the eerie silence remains, you still have hope. He wants you to know you still have God. He wants you to be still. 🌿

WHERE WERE YOU?

> WHERE WERE YOU WHEN I LAID THE
> FOUNDATIONS OF THE EARTH? TELL ME, IF
> YOU KNOW SO MUCH. DO YOU KNOW HOW
> ITS DIMENSIONS WERE DETERMINED AND
> WHO DID THE SURVEYING? WHAT SUPPORTS
> ITS FOUNDATIONS, AND WHO LAID ITS
> CORNERSTONE AS THE MORNING STARS
> SANG TOGETHER AND ALL THE ANGELS
> SHOUTED FOR JOY?
> *Job 38:4–7*

I was thirteen years old when a childhood friend lost her mother to breast cancer. I remember standing up in confirmation class demanding an explanation. Why would a loving God allow such suffering? Job wondered too. So did his friends. Job was a righteous man who loved God. He lived a life of wealth and prestige until suddenly, everything was stripped away. His livestock, servants, farmhands, home, and all his children were destroyed (Job 1:13–19). Then, if things weren't bad enough, he was struck with a terrible case of boils from head to foot (Job 2:7).

In his deep suffering, Job cursed the day of his birth. He felt it was better to never be born than forsaken by God. He wondered why his world had crumbled despite his right living. His friends insisted that sin had caused his suffering and urged him to repent. But Job maintained his innocence (Job 3–31). Finally the Lord spoke to Job from a mighty whirlwind. He didn't give Job any answers. Instead, He asked a series of questions Job couldn't possibly answer. *Where were you when I laid the foundations of the earth?*

If Job's human mind couldn't grasp the wonder of God's physical creation, how could he possibly understand God's mind and character (Job 38–41)? Job responded by humbling himself before God (Job 42:1–6). And God restored him to happiness and health, giving him twice as much as he had before (Job 42:10–16).

Sometimes I feel thirteen all over again. I'm tempted to stomp my feet and demand an answer. *Why, God?* Sometimes suffering prepares us for a higher calling. Sometimes it's an attack by Satan. Sometimes, like Job, we simply don't know why we suffer. Job let his need to know why consume him. But God made it clear. It's better to know Him than to know why. As Job learned, when everything else is stripped away, God is all we ever had. He's all we'll ever need. And those who endure testing will experience His great rewards (Hebrews 10:35–36).

As you face your cancer today, you can curse God and give up. Or you can trust God and draw near. Where were you? Where was I? We weren't there as the morning stars sang together and all the angels shouted for joy. God's ways and God's thoughts are higher than ours (Isaiah 55:8–9). No standard of authority is higher than His. Choose to trust Him. Choose to submit to His sovereignty and rest in His loving arms. He will never leave you or forsake you (Hebrews 13:5). He is God. And He's enough. *

A Different Kind of Medicine

> PAY ATTENTION, MY CHILD, TO WHAT I SAY.
> LISTEN CAREFULLY. DON'T LOSE SIGHT OF
> MY WORDS. LET THEM PENETRATE DEEP
> WITHIN YOUR HEART, FOR THEY BRING LIFE
> AND RADIANT HEALTH TO ANYONE WHO
> DISCOVERS THEIR MEANING.
> *Proverbs 4:20–22*

If it had to happen, there isn't a better time in history to get breast cancer. After years of research and medical breakthroughs, there is hope on the horizon. Early detection methods and innovative drugs for prevention and treatment continue to dramatically increase the survival rates for women with breast cancer. Women who suffered thirty years ago weren't so fortunate. Doctors discovered the cancer too late, performed radical mastectomies, and crossed their fingers.

In the midst of all this innovation, there's a different kind of medicine. It's been around since the beginning of time. It treats every human need. Like all medicines, it works only when we follow the instructions. When applied directly to the heart and allowed to penetrate deeply, it promises to bring life and radiant health to anyone who uses it properly. This medicine is the Word of God. You can start taking it immediately and you don't need a prescription. You'll find it readily available in the pages of the Holy Bible. Here are a few sample doses to get you started on the road to divine health:

- "If you will listen carefully to the voice of the Lord your God and do what is right in his sight, obeying his commands and laws, then I will not make you suffer . . . for I am the Lord who heals you" (Exodus 15:26).
- "But in that coming day, no weapon turned against you will succeed" (Isaiah 54:17).
- "If you do these things, your salvation will come like the dawn. Yes, your healing will come quickly. Your godliness will lead you forward, and the glory of the Lord will protect you from behind" (Isaiah 58:8).
- "'I will give you back your health and heal your wounds,' says the Lord" (Jeremiah 30:17).
- "O Lord my God, I cried out to you for help, and you restored my health" (Psalm 30:2).
- "Praise the Lord, I tell myself, and never forget the good things he does for me. He forgives all my sins and heals all my diseases" (Psalm 103:2–3).
- "He spoke, and they were healed—snatched from the door of death" (Psalm 107:20).
- "Are any among you sick? They should call for the elders of the church and have them pray over them, anointing them with oil in the name of the Lord. And their prayer offered in faith will heal the sick, and the Lord will make them well" (James 5:14–15).
- "He personally carried away our sins in his own body on the cross so we can be dead to sin and live for what is right. You have been healed by his wounds" (1 Peter 2:24)!
- "So if you are suffering according to God's will, keep on doing what is right, and trust yourself to the God who made you, for he will never fail you" (1 Peter 4:19).

Unlike others on the market, this medicine has pleasant side effects. In fact, the more you take, the better you feel. You'll find it palatable. It tastes sweeter than honey. It improves your vision so you never have to stumble around in the dark again. And when you apply it properly to your daily life, it makes you wise (Psalm 119:97–105). Best of all, it has no shelf life. Other medicines come and go. Human knowledge changes like the wind. But the Word of God stands forever (Isaiah 40:8). Apply it liberally to the affected area. You'll be amazed at the results. ❧

GRACE FOR EACH HOUR

> GOD SAVED YOU BY HIS SPECIAL FAVOR
> WHEN YOU BELIEVED. AND YOU CAN'T TAKE
> CREDIT FOR THIS; IT IS A GIFT FROM GOD.
> SALVATION IS NOT A REWARD FOR THE
> GOOD THINGS WE HAVE DONE, SO NONE OF
> US CAN BOAST ABOUT IT.
> *Ephesians 2:8–9*

It's finally over—the long drawn-out diagnosis, the surgery, five months of chemo, six weeks of daily radiation treatments—all over. On that last day, I drove away from the radiation clinic experiencing a full range of emotions . . . elation, contentment, overwhelming relief . . . others too difficult to name. Even so, there was a little tug deep in my soul. *What now, Lord?* As I pulled up to a stoplight, I noticed the song playing on the radio. It was something about being blessed. In all the worst times and the best, the woman singing was blessed. If she were never again to climb a mountain or stand on the ocean shore, she was blessed. The Lord gave her joy, love, and strength and never left her side. She was blessed. And so was I. It was a revelation moment. An understanding of the depth of God's amazing grace exploded in my spirit. If God took me home that very day, I am blessed. I have a rich and full life on this earth and the promise of living in eternity with Him in a place so awesome no human mind can imagine it (1 Corinthians 2:9).

What is this amazing grace? It's God's unmerited favor toward us . . . the unearned, undeserved gifts He pours out on His children. His grace brought me peace during every hour of my cancer journey (Philippians 4:7). His grace blesses me with riches from heaven (Deuteronomy 28:1–14). His grace fills me completely with faith and love (1 Timothy 1:14). His grace gives me the strength to face each new day (2 Corinthians 12:9). It was by His grace I woke up every day before my breast cancer, and it will be by His grace I wake up every day after. His grace saved me from destruction and promises a life of abundance in this world and the next.

Oh Lord, who am I that you would bless me like this? (2 Samuel 7:18). I'm just an ordinary person. But I'm saved by God's grace. It's a free gift so none can boast. I can't earn it. It doesn't depend on my record of good deeds, and it certainly doesn't depend on the bad things I've done. If it did, the apostle Paul would never have become the greatest faith hero in history. He murdered Christians before he met Christ. He called himself the worst sinner of all. And he never forgot he was saved by grace (1 Timothy 1:15–16).

God's gracious favor is upon you. His richest blessings belong to you. All you have to do is ask. *Lord, I need you. I know you love me and have a perfect plan for my life, even during this breast cancer. I know I have fallen short. Thank you for sending your Son to die on the cross for my sins. I open my heart and receive you as my Lord and Savior. Thank you for loving me so much that you forgive my sins and give me eternal life. Lord, I surrender my life to you. Please pour your blessing on me. Please make me the person you created me to be.* And now, dear sister, may your Father in heaven give you grace for each hour, grace for each day, and grace forevermore. ❦

SCRIPTURE INDEX

He Hears You Knocking,
Luke 11:9–10

Unleash the Power,
James 5:14–15

May I Have Your Attention
Please?
Romans 9:20–21

Only God,
Psalm 44:5–7

The Inner Circle,
Philippians 3:8

Daughter of the King,
Hebrews 4:16

Love Letter From Heaven,
Isaiah 40:8

Set in Stone,
Malachi 3:6

Biker Chick,
2 Corinthians 3:16–17

Nothing to Fear,
Psalm 46:1–3

Coats of Pride,
1 Peter 5:5–6

Totally Unconditional,
1 Corinthians 13:4–7

New Tires,
Isaiah 40:29–31

A Million Miles Away,
Psalm 22:1–3

No Escape,
Psalm 139:7–12

Hazardous to Your Health,
Psalm 41:6–8

Throw Away the Key,
2 Corinthians 10:5

God Breathed,
2 Timothy 3:16–17

Let the Party Begin!
Luke 15:21–24

The God of Your Parking Place,
Psalm 37:23–24

Done Deal,
Romans 3:27–28

He Conquered Every One,
John 16:33

Blessings From Heaven,
Deuteronomy 28:2–6

Your Power Source,
2 Corinthians 4:7

Holy Ground,
Mark 15:37–38

A Child's Faith,
Mark 10:13–15

Thank You, Lord!
Psalm 92:1–4

Dare to Believe,
Romans 4:17

Woman, Why Are You Crying?
John 20:11–16

He Never Sleeps,
Psalm 121

Holy Hot Flash,
Acts 2:1–4

Not Mine,
Psalm 24:1

Rescue Me!
Isaiah 43:1–3